What students are saying:

"Thank you for following up. I just wanted to share the good news that I will be attending the Elson S. Floyd School of Medicine [Washington State University Medical School] in the fall. It was the last interview I did, and I used BeMo to prep for it. I spoke with the dean of admissions and she said the I did much better on my MMI than the majority of applicants, so I am super happy with the help that I got from BeMo!" – Shreya

"I was accepted to 5 out of 6! - F. Edward Herbert School of Medicine - University of Vermont College of Medicine - Cooper Medical School of Rowan University - Oakland University of William Beaumont School of Medicine - Rutgers Robert Wood Johnson Medical School." – Ada

"I think your interview [MMI] prep made a great impact on my preparation! I got accepted to UC Davis, Georgetown, UC Riverside (full scholarship - matriculating), Loma Linda, and UCLA. I've thus far recommended your site to anyone I meet. – Marysia

"Just wanted to drop you a line and let you know that I was accepted into all three schools (Queen's, Mac and U of T) but will be accepting U of T. Thanks again for all the help in the process [application review, CASPer prep & MMI prep] and I look forward to seeing you around campus / hospitals in the near future. Cheers," – Sameer

"Hello, The interviews went great, thanks again for all the help [with CASPer & MMI prep]! I was accepted to McMaster, Queen's, and NOSM [medical schools]. Thanks again," – Jesse

"Thank you for your assistance in preparing me with the CASPer and MMI interviews! I wanted to let you know that I was accepted at Robert Wood Johnson Medical School! Please extend my thanks to the instructors who helped me prepare. Thanks again," – Jason

"I was accepted to the University of Vermont (UVM) and Quinnipiac (Frank H. Netter MD School of Medicine at Quinnipiac University) and will be going to UVM in the fall, which I'm very excited about! I appreciate all the help BeMo provided me in preparing for my interview!!" – Danielle

"Thanks for checking in. Yes, the interviews went really well - I got into all the universities I interviewed at (Toronto, McMaster, and Northern)! " – Megan

"I have heard back from all the schools I applied to. I was accepted at 6 different veterinary schools: Texas A&M, Midwestern, Mississippi State, Oklahoma State, Penn, and Cornell. I was initially waitlisted at Penn and Cornell. Texas A&M conducted an MMI style interview, while Midwestern, Mississippi State, and Penn had traditional interviews. I will be attending my in-state school, Texas A&M, starting in August. Thank you for all your help!" – Callie

"Thanks for the message. The application process went really well, and I am excited to be attending Columbia University College of Physicians and Surgeons in the fall. Thank you for your help," – Andy

"Good News! I was accepted to all three medical schools where I interviewed: University of Toronto, University of Ottawa, and Albert Einstein College of Medicine. I have officially accepted my offer to U of T... Thanks again for all your help! I was very pleased with the service I received." – Joanna

"Hello! My interviews went great actually. I was accepted at NYMC and UMass Medical School, both of which had MMI interview format. I will be attending UMass in the fall. Both my mock interviews gave me really good preparation and the interviewers were wonderful! So I certainly owe a lot of credit to BeMo for helping me reach my goals :) I'd be happy to write a testimonial, etc. Thank you," – Nate

"I hope you are well. I've received acceptances from the University of Toronto, University of Saskatchewan, and University of British Columbia and I'm on

the waitlisted at the University of Ottawa. I think BeMo definitely helped prepare me! I'm very grateful for those who helped me improve and prepare."
– Saloni

"Thank you for your email. I'll be attending UCSD in the fall. Thank you for the support and resources!" – Jessica

BeMo's Ultimate Guide to Multiple Mini Interview (MMI)

How to Increase Your MMI SIM Score by 27% without Memorizing any Sample Questions

BeMo® Academic Consulting Inc.

ISBN: 1729763367

ISBN 13: 978-1729763360

Important Notice. Please read carefully. By using this book, you acknowledge that you have read, understood, and agreed with our terms and conditions below.

Disclaimer: Please note that certain parts of this book are similar or identical to the content presented in BeMo's interview video training course and BeMo's Ultimate Guide to Medical School Admissions. If you have purchased BeMo's video course or one of our Multiple Mini Interview (MMI) preparation programs, you will have access to most of the content presented, although certain parts of this book are completely new material and are not included in our video course or MMI preparation programs. Furthermore, if you have purchased any of our CASPer prep video training, programs or book, you will notice several similarities. This is because CASPer is very similar to MMI and in fact it was created by the same university. Nevertheless, there are many differences which we have highlighted in this book. Moreover, doing well on CASPer does not necessarily translate to doing well on MMI or vice versa. You may choose to use this book as a starting point in your preparation or as a complement to our MMI programs at your discretion.

We have conducted thorough research to provide accurate information to help you prepare for and ace your MMI. However, readers are responsible for their own results and must always adhere to official instructions.

BeMo is not affiliated with, nor endorses, any of the organizations mentioned including, but not limited to, universities, colleges, official test administrators or any external websites, unless explicitly indicated otherwise.

Score increase claims refer to MMI score increase in practice simulations.

LIST OF CONTRIBUTING AUTHORS

Dr. Behrouz Moemeni, Ph.D., founder & CEO @ BeMo

Ms. Ronza Nissan, M.A., admissions expert & lead trainer

Dr. Sarah Lynn Kleeb, Ph.D., admissions expert

Dr. Veena Netrakanti, M.D., admissions expert.

Dr. Kyle Paradis, Ph.D., admissions expert

Dr. Andrej Arsovski, Ph.D., admissions expert & senior scientist

Dr. Karim Wafa, M.D., admissions expert

Dr. Jenifer Truong, M.D., admissions expert

Dr. Lauren Colbert, M.D., admissions expert

Want a FREE sample Simulated mock MMI?

Go to BeMoSampleMMI.com

Would you like us to help you ace MMI?

Go to BeMoMMI.com

Contents

Acknowledgments:

We would like to thank our students and their parents for putting their trust in us and giving us the privilege to be part of their journey. You have inspired us and taught us lessons we would not have learned on our own. Thank you for your continued support and for investing in our mission. You are the reason we get up in the morning.

We would like to thank the countless number of admissions deans, directors, officers, pre-health advisors and school counselors who have "unofficially" supported our mission. Thank you for encouraging us and, most importantly, thank you for making us think critically. We appreciate what you do, and we understand the impossible task you face each and every single day.

A huge thanks to our team members, both past and present. BeMo wouldn't be what it is today without you.

And, of course, a huge thanks to our family and friends who have been unconditionally supportive, even when we couldn't spend as much time with them because of our obsession with our mission here at BeMo.

Foreword

First, CONGRATULATIONS for making the commitment to educate yourself to become not only a competitive applicant, but also a better person, and as a result, a better future professional. The fact that you have purchased this book tells us that you understand the value of continuous learning and self-improvement. The world rewards individuals who continuously seek to educate themselves because "knowledge is power." Before we get into the details, we need to set the record straight about why you should listen to us, what this book is all about, who this book is for, and who it is NOT for, but first, a few words from our founder and CEO.

Why I Founded BeMo®: Message from BeMo's Founder and CEO, Dr. Behrouz Moemeni

Sometimes you must do what's important, even if the chances of success are slim to none.

Students often ask me what motivated me to found BeMo and what gets me up in the morning.

The answer for me is rather simple and has remained the same since day one.

I started BeMo with my cofounder, Dr. Mo Bayegan, in 2013 as a company - see why it's called "BeMo" now? - but the duo that came to be BeMo really started when we first met back in high school in 1996, and then later solidified during our undergraduate and graduate training years.

We both felt every student deserves access to higher education, regardless of his or her social status or cultural background, because education is the best way to introduce positive change in our world.

Sadly, I believe most of the current admissions practices, tools and procedures are not necessarily fair, are mostly out-dated, and more importantly, remain scientifically unproven. Therefore, in 2013, as Mo and I were finishing our graduate studies, we decided to create BeMo to make sure no one is treated unfairly because of flawed admission practices.

At the time, I was finishing my Ph.D. studies in the field of Immunology at the University of Toronto, which was a transformational educational experience. I had the privilege to work with one of the sharpest minds in the field, Dr. Michael Julius. He taught me many things over the years and two lessons stayed with me: 1) the tremendous value of curiosity in scientific or technological innovation to seek the truth rather than confirming one's own opinions 2) whatever you do has to be the reason that gets you up in the morning. I admit that I wasn't the best student he could have had, but I had a relatively successful time as a Ph.D. student. I won 19 awards and I was invited to 7 international conferences. I was even offered an unsolicited job before I had defended my thesis. The job offered a secure source of income and I would have been able to start paying my mounting student loan debt, but I decided to abandon a career in academia in favor of starting BeMo. Despite the uncertainty, many well-established competitors, and lack of secure source of income, I felt - and I still do - that the mission was well worth the risk, even if the probability of success seemed infinitely slim. I truly believe what we do here at BeMo adds more value to each of our students' lives than anything else I could have done, and I would not trade it for the world.

Over the years, we have been fortunate enough to help many students and have an amazing and steadily growing team. We really couldn't have done it without them and it's been a privilege to teach with them and learn from them over the years (thanks for sticking with us!).

We are aware that our methods have been controversial in some circles; innovative ideas often are. However, we are confident in our belief - and the scientific literature supports this - that current admissions practices are rife with bias and must be improved.

In fact, in 2017, I founded another independent company called SortSmart®, which has created what I consider to be the fairest, most scientifically sound and cost-effective admissions screening tool out there. I invite you to visit SortSmart.io to learn more and tell your university admissions office to bring SortSmart to your school.

In the meantime, while SortSmart is gathering momentum, at BeMo, we will continue to support students just like you to make sure no groups of students are treated unfairly. You can rest assured that there is no stopping us.

To your success,

Behrouz Moemeni, Ph.D.

CEO @ BeMo

Here's A Bit About Us: BeMo Academic Consulting ("BeMo") BeMoAcademicConsulting.com

We're an energetic academic consulting firm, comprised of a team of researchers and professionals who use a proven, evidence-based, and scientific approach to help prospective students with career path development and admissions to undergraduate, graduate, and professional programs such as medicine, law, dentistry, and pharmacy.

We believe your education is one of your most valuable assets and learning how to become a great future professional or scholar doesn't need to be complicated. We also believe that every student deserves access to higher education, regardless of his or her social status or cultural background. However, in our opinion, most of the current admissions practices, tools and procedures are not necessarily fair, are often outdated, and more importantly, remain scientifically unproven.

Our goal is to create truly useful (and scientifically sound) programs and tools that work and provide more than just some trivial information like the other "admissions consulting companies" out there. We want to make sure everyone has a fair chance of admission to highly competitive professional programs despite current biased admissions practices.

We do whatever it takes to come up with creative solutions and then implement like mad scientists. We're passionate about mentoring our students. We're obsessed with delivering useful educational programs and we go where others dare not to explore.

Why should you listen to us?

Our primary area of focus is preparation of applicants for extremely competitive professional schools. Specifically, we are the leaders in CASPer preparation, multiple mini interview (MMI) preparation, traditional interview preparation, video interview preparation and application review. We have an exceptional team of practicing professionals, medical doctors, scholars, and scientists who have served as former MMI evaluators and admissions committee members (visit our website, BeMoAcademicConsulting.com to learn more about our admissions experts). To give you an idea, each year we help thousands of students gain admission to top schools around the world. What we are about to share is based on what we have learned in our much sought-after one-on-one coaching programs. What we offer works and it works consistently. In fact our MMI preparation programs have been proven to significantly increase applicants' MMI practice scores by 27%. Our programs are in high demand and we are certain they will also work for you, as well.

Why did we write this book?

In our opinion, there is so much misinformation around admissions processes, both online and offline – from online forums to university clubs and even some university guidance counselors and official test administrators. While some of these sources are well-intended (though not all are well-intended), the level of misinformation is astounding. For example, in our opinion, most online forums cannot be trusted because it is not clear who the authors are or what motivates them, and thus their credibility comes into question. These forums are frequently filled with fake profiles; some of those fake profiles are official university administrators and test administrators trying to control the flow of information, so only their version of "facts" is distributed. To make matters worse, some of these forums offer "sponsorship opportunities" to companies, which puts them in a financial conflict of interest. Most student clubs are also to be avoided, because they also frequently form financial relationships with companies in order to support their operations and, as such, they receive and distribute one-sided information. Additionally, most books out there are incomplete and tend to have a narrow focus on teaching you 'tricks' about MMI, without offering any meaningful strategy on how to ace any possible *type* of MMI question. They do not focus on the big picture that is essential to your success, both as an applicant and as a future practicing professional.

What is this book about?

This book is about the big picture. It is about how to develop into a mature, ethical, and knowledgeable individual, which is essential to becoming a future practicing professional. While we spend a considerable amount of time walking you through specific instructions on how to prepare for MMI, it is important to always remain focused on the big picture.

Who is this book for and who is it NOT for?

If you are applying to any program that requires you to participate in a multiple mini interview, then this is perfect for you. Regardless of where you start, this book has something for you, provided that you are willing to put in the hard work and invest in yourself. Getting into a competitive professional school is challenging, as is becoming a practicing professional. In fact, the journey is both very difficult and very expensive in terms of time, money, and energy. We do NOT share any quick 'tricks', 'shortcuts', or 'insider' scoops like some of the other books out there. Therefore, this book is NOT for anyone who is looking for an easy, cheap, shortcut to get in.

We do not share any such tricks or shortcuts because:

A) There are no tricks or insider info that can help you, because you cannot trick your way to becoming a mature, ethical professional. Rather, you must put in long hours of self-training. Think of it this way: if a professional athlete must train for years - on average ten years, hence the "ten-year rule" - to get to that level of proficiency, wouldn't it make sense that our future doctors, teachers, nurses, and dentists, who deal with people's lives, would need to put in the effort to learn the skills required?

B) Sharing 'tricks' or 'insider scoops' would be highly unethical and against our philosophy of what constitutes a mature professional. You should be immediately alarmed if a book or admissions company claims to be sharing 'insider' information.

C) We have a strict policy at BeMo to only help students who are genuinely interested in becoming a caring future professional and helping their community, rather than those who may be primarily motivated by financial security, status, or social pressure from their parents and peers.

How should you read this book?

We recommend that you first read the book cover to cover and then come back to specific chapters for a detailed read. The more you read the book, the more you internalize the essential strategies that you may have missed. It is important to note that there is a lot of information in this book, and if you try to do everything at once, it may seem overwhelming and discouraging. Therefore, it is best that you first read this book for pleasure from cover to cover, and then take one or two points from one of the chapters and gradually start to implement our recommendations.

To your success,

Your friends at BeMo

CHAPTER I

What is the Multiple Mini Interview (MMI)?

The Multiple Mini Interview, commonly abbreviated as "MMI", is a situational judgment test type interview, modeled after the objective structured clinical examination (OSCE). OSCE is an examination used to evaluate clinical performance of health care professional trainees, such as students in medicine, nursing, physician assistant, pharmacy, and dentistry. It is designed to test students' skills in multiple independent stations mimicking future real-life scenarios that students may face in interacting with patients as practicing professionals. In an OSCE, students move from short stations lasting 5-10 minutes, while interacting with real or simulated patients; their performance is evaluated by one or two independent examiners at each station. An MMI is similarly structured to include multiple short stations where applicants are assessed based on their response to hypothetical everyday scenarios. The interview consists of anywhere between 6 to

12 stations, each lasting 4 to 8 minutes, and may take approximately 2 hours to complete.

History and rationale behind the use of MMI

Before we discuss the history and rationale for the use of MMI, we need to examine the origin of professional school interviews. Incidentally, the first such interview was introduced as part of medical school admissions; as such, our discussion will begin with the founding of the first medical school.

The first medical school, Schola Medica Salernitana, was founded in the 9th century in southern Italy. It appears that the only people admitted to this school were those who could financially afford eight years of medical training – and remarkably, this is still the observed trend to this date, despite the use of different admissions criteria, as you will see shortly. The admissions criteria were based merely on the financial status of the applicants, rather than previous academic success, critical reasoning, or interpersonal skills. Although finances determined admissions, Schola Medica Salernitana published several guides about treating patients respectfully – including patient care and bedside manner. This indicates that, since the inception of medical training, the healthcare profession has always been based on patient care and bedside manner, regardless of admissions criteria.

Moving forward in time, and in the context of North America, the first medical school, the Perelman School of Medicine, was pioneered by the University of Pennsylvania. The Perelman School of Medicine, and other institutions that opened around that time, maintained the basic principles established by the Schola Medica Salernitana – the importance of being of service to others and the need for equal emphasis on both technical and interpersonal skills. However, the medical schools that were opening in North America based their admission criteria on previous academic success because they wanted to train students who already had the foundations and skills necessary to complete their studies, along with having a suitable bedside manner. Interpersonal skills were thought to be developed during medical school training.

It wasn't until the 1920s that standardized testing was included in the admission process. The original test, created by F.A. Moss and colleagues, was at first called the "Moss Test", and was later revamped and renamed as the "Medical College Admissions Test", commonly referred to as the MCAT. The MCAT was thought to be a measure of readiness for medical school. The problem was that accepting students based on standardized testing and academic history lead to attrition rates that were as high as 50%. The response to high attrition was to increase academic requirements, in addition to standardized testing.

In the late 90s and early 2000s, professional regulatory bodies of medicine began conducting studies to understand the major complaints that the public has about their healthcare professionals. This led to a study in the *New England Journal of Medicine* which revealed that the number one complaint most patients had about their physicians was not with regard to their clinical skills and competencies, but rather with the doctors' emotional intelligence and soft skills (N Engl J Med 2005; 353:2673-2682). For example, patients complained that their doctors weren't compassionate or empathetic enough, or simply did not have good communications skills. Based on this evidence, professional faculties were asked to devise admissions procedures that selected candidates who not only had a great academic record, but also possessed strong soft skills.

To comply with this and to improve the admissions process, many professional faculties began utilizing various tools to find appropriate candidates who possess strong soft skills. Soft skills include traits such as communication skills, teamwork, empathy, critical thinking, ethical decision making, inter-personal relations, and professionalism. The evaluative tools that were initially introduced were: the personal statement, autobiographical sketch, short essays, and the traditional interview. With regard to the professional school interview and the most up-and-coming interview style, in 2002 McMaster's Faculty of Medicine began to develop the Multiple Mini Interview – commonly abbreviated as "MMI". The developers claim that each mini interview is designed to mimic situations that students or practicing professionals may encounter, or to target a skill that you need to draw upon when you begin practicing as a professional. As such, the MMI was initially developed to mimic clinical Objective Structured Clinical Evaluation (OSCE) exams and board exams.

Research by Dahlin and colleagues (2012), has shown that candidates who are selected by their interview performance, rather than their academic qualifications alone, have performed better on the Objective Structured Clinical Examination. Because practical clinical exams are designed in a format very similar to the MMI, the MMI gives an indication of whether or not you have the capacity to go from situation to situation (much like you would in a real clinical setting) and perform well, regardless of how the previous station transpired. In certain situations, during an MMI, the admissions committee may purposely make one of the stations drastically difficult from the others, with the intention of flustering candidates, so that they are able to assess your ability to perform well in such stressful situations. Essentially, they are testing your ability to move on from a previous mistake and into a new situation, and to do so successfully. As you can likely imagine, once you are a practicing professional, you may have to interact with 20-30 patients on a daily basis. Let's assume one of the patients is having a very bad day and your interaction with him or her does not go according to plan. What will you do? Will you allow that interaction to interfere with the way you interact with the remainder of your patients or colleagues? Or, will you let go of that unfortunate experience and approach the remainder of your cases objectively and with a new, positive outlook?

In theory, the MMIs are claimed to standardize applicant interview content, decrease perceived bias, increase the total number of applicants to be interviewed, and increase inter-rater reliability, as there are multiple samplings of your personality across 8-12 various stations, reviewed by 8-12 different interviewers. With regard to undergraduate medical school applicants, research has reported that performance on the MMI is a "statistically significant predictor" of success in undergraduate medical school training, and specifically during the early years. Moreover, applicants who have high performance on MMIs have been reported to likewise perform effectively on national licensing exams for medicine.

Although some professional schools have been making a shift from traditional panel interviews to MMIs, it is important to acknowledge that the research literature does show conflicting arguments that should be acknowledged.

For example, Soares and colleagues (2015) conducted a study comparing MMIs with traditional panel interviews for US emergency medicine residency applicants. The participants in this study were part of the 2011-2012 interview season for emergency room medical residency positions in the US. The applicants expressed that the MMI was less enjoyable, when compared to traditional interviews, and they felt that it was more difficult to portray themselves accurately, as they had to address a preselected scenario as opposed to discussing their personal achievements and experiences, as in a traditional panel interview. The authors of the study acknowledge that the results may have been due to the applicants' lack of familiarity with the MMI structure. In light of the research findings, the results from this study are telling because they acknowledge that showing your soft skills in an MMI can be more difficult than in traditional panel interviews, because of the type of questions being asked. Now, recall that MMIs were originally developed to evaluate candidates largely on their emotional intelligence and soft skills, in part to better predict the quality of your future clinical practice. As such, you need to prepare thoroughly and effectively for your MMI so that you can address the questions in a clear, organized, and succinct manner AND portray your soft skills. To be able to do this, you need to practice and prepare for these interviews ahead of time with a coach who can ensure you possess all the key elements needed for a successful interview.

Let's take some time to go into more detail about the issue of reliability when discussing interviews. Regardless of the interview type, either MMI or traditional panel, there will always be questions regarding how accurately interviewers assess soft attributes of the applicants, as such attributes tend to be subjective or qualitative in nature, as opposed to the quantitative evaluations provided by standardized tests. For example, discrepancies between interviewers' evaluations may stem from inconsistent interviewer training, differences in experience as an interviewer, and longstanding – potentially unconscious – biases. As with all interviews, there is a human element that needs to be considered, but that human element may be evaluated or prioritized differently when selecting the "best" candidates. In fact, in their 1996 paper, "Factors Affecting the Selection of Students for Medical School", researchers Harasym and colleagues identified that the variability between interviewers can account for up to 56% of the total variance in interview ratings. More specifically, these biases reduce objectivity when making decisions because the biases can lead evaluators to make quick decisions, to be overly enthusiastic in justifying personal decisions, and to selectively search for evidence to support their judgment, rather than objectively evaluating all information equally to make judgment.

MMIs are claimed to be used amongst several professional schools for the following reasons:

- First, interpersonal skills and professionalism are universally required. The act of listening, communicating, being able to present ideas, resolve conflict, foster an open and honest environment, build and maintain professional relationships, act as a team member, and make conscientious ethically and legally sound decisions, are all crucial skills for your future success. You also need to be approachable, friendly, caring, and attentive to others' actions, words, and desires – regardless of the specific profession you enter.

- Second, all service professions have a common set of professional values. MMIs test the interviewees' ability to put the patient's needs before their own, to approach complex problems, to avoid jumping to conclusions or making assumptions, to understand your role within a system, to reach out to others for assistance, and to reach ethical decisions.

- Third, MMI stations aim to see the way you *approach* and *work through* problems, even more so than your final answers. This greatly targets your communication skills, as you must be able to articulate your thinking process.

We'll end this section with an interesting fact about the MMI. The rights for MMI appear to have been acquired by a for-profit company out of McMaster, called the Professional Fit Assessment

Tool for Human Resources experts, or ProFitHR for short. According to the ProFitHR website, ProFitHR is a "spin-off company" from McMaster University's research and development of the MMI. It seems to have been created so that the shareholders of the company could capitalize on selling the MMI concept to "professional schools and corporations around the world".

So, you may be asking, "What? The researchers and university who claim MMI is best are the same ones profiting from it?" The short and simple answer is, "Yes". How's that for a conflict of interest? In fact, wouldn't this make a fantastic sample MMI question?

Do situational judgment tests really work?

Before we haste into specific preparation strategies, we need to take a closer look at situational judgment tests, because this will provide you with a greater depth of understanding of such tests. The more background knowledge you have, the better you can prepare for these tests, because you will know the larger purpose of the test and this will help in structuring your responses.

Remember, the MMI (and its online twin sister, CASPer) is merely a situational judgment test, or SJT. SJTs utilize an outdated methodology that has been around for decades, especially in the workforce for hiring new employees. SJTs work by placing applicants in hypothetical real-life scenarios and evaluating their on-the-spot behaviors. The assumption is that this methodology gives a better indication of the applicants' true behaviors, priorities, and tendencies.

However, in our opinion, there are multiple problems with SJTs such as MMI (and CASPer) as follows:

Problem #1:

The use of hypothetical scenarios may force applicants to provide hypothetical responses. The applicants know that the only way to do well is to provide a hypothetical response that is socially acceptable. Therefore, instead of providing what they *really* would have done, they provide what they think is going to get them accepted. This means that such tests might not be able to discern the true personality of applicants; rather, they can merely detect applicants' ability to formulate hypothetical responses to hypothetical situations, at best.

Problem #2:

Applicants coming from a higher socioeconomic background appear to be better able to formulate a socially acceptable response due to their upbringing and socialization, putting others at a disadvantage. In fact, two independent studies of medical school admissions in the United States and Canada, conducted by SortSmart, showed that all admissions screening tools, including MMI, appear to be more likely to select applicants coming from higher income families.

Family Income of Medical School Applicants

Selected with Different Admissions Tests

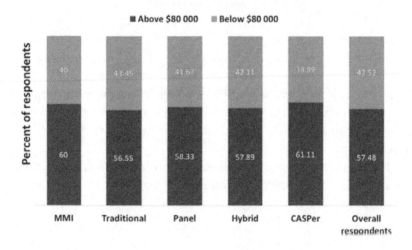

Figure 1. The Wealthy are the Most Represented Group Regardless of the Admissions Tool Used to Select Them. Printed with permission from SortSmart Candidate Selection Inc.

A survey of American medical school students and residents showed that the majority of selected applicants ("overall respondents") came from high income families earning more than $80,000/year, while the median household income in the United States is ~$60,000/year, according to the U.S. Census Bureau. The results further indicated that there are no significant differences between the percentage of wealthy applicants in the overall pool of respondents and the pools of respondents selected using the various admissions tools highlighted. This is similar to other published reports indicating that applicants with higher socioeconomic status appear to score higher on situational judgment tests, as compared to those with lower socioeconomic status and those from underrepresented minorities. (See: Acad Med. 2015 Dec; 90(12):1667-74. doi: 10.1097/ACM.0000000000000766, which can be found at https://www.ncbi.nlm.nih.gov/pubmed/26017355)

Judging the appropriateness of a response to a very delicate or stressful hypothetical scenario can also vary across cultures. These tests are singularly guided by accepted western cultural norms. This can pose significant challenges to non-native applicants, new immigrants, or those who are immersed in another culture. The diverse cultural makeup of the United States, the United Kingdom, Australia, and Canada, for example, makes this a significant issue for applicants. Evidently, at the 2016 medical education conference in Canada, the New York Medical College (NYMC) reported that underrepresented minority applicants scored lower on CASPer (online version of the MMI), and that males scored lower than females, indicating a possible gender bias, as well. Furthermore, published research has likewise demonstrated that the MMI appears to cause bias against male applicants, and underrepresented minority groups score lower on these types of interviews, as well. You can find the two studies at the following URLs:

https://www.ncbi.nlm.nih.gov/pubmed/28557950

https://www.ncbi.nlm.nih.gov/pubmed/26017355

Problem #3:

The claim that these tests are "immune to test preparation" is a difficult one to accept. The tests aim to assess personal and professional characteristics, qualities that any good parent or education system aims to instill in its pupils. With knowledge of the professional values exalted by a given discipline, students can absolutely work with a coach or mentor to refine the kinds of qualities that reflect such values, making them more competitive applicants. Furthermore, as you will see shortly, we have evidence that proves coaching can and does impact performance.

Personal and professional behaviors are not inherited but learned; claiming otherwise is irresponsible and can amount to discrimination.

Problem #4:

SJTs have not been validated to correlate with actual on-the-job behavior and the best correlation found to date has been self-reported by the creators of the for-profit companies selling these products. In their pilot study, the company's founders report a low correlation of a mere $r = 0.37–0.39$ between MMI scores and test scores in future medical licensing examinations. First, the study seems to suffer from the law of small numbers and confidence over doubt bias because of its small sample sizes and the conflict of interest by the authors and the host university. Second, note that a) the test is merely a predictor of future test performance, not future on-the-job behavior, and b) the correlation is weak at best because of a correlation factor of about 0.4. Briefly, correlation factor or "r value" can range from 0 - meaning zero correlation between two variables - and 1 – meaning 100% correlation between two variables. Therefore, r value of 0.4 translates to the ability to explain 16% of the variance between the two variables. Imagine going to a doctor who claimed to be able to make a correct diagnosis 16% of the time!

Problem #5:

SJTs are unable to measure the level of motivation of each applicant. Motivation is important because motivation directs behavior, not test scores. Furthermore, motivation is not correlated with gender, race, or socioeconomic status.

The point is this: you must question everything. All the time. Never take anything at face value, even if it comes from "official" sources. Best practices change and evolve continuously as new discoveries are made. This is relevant from treatment options for illnesses to admissions practices. Progress has been driven by those who have an insatiable appetite to continuously push the status quo, by those who have an aversion to the phrase "because it has always been done that way." For example, Galileo was mocked, ridiculed, and imprisoned because he refused to believe the accepted dogma that Earth is the center of the universe because he had scientific evidence that suggested otherwise. Many years later, his work was praised by Albert Einstein and Galileo eventually came to be known as the father of modern physics.

Marcus Aurelius said it best almost 2000 years ago: "Everything we hear is an opinion, not a fact. Everything we see is a perspective, not the truth."

This attitude is paramount to our future as a society. As a future professional, you have the responsibility to push the boundary of current "truths" and advance new discoveries and improvements. Most discoveries are proven incorrect as new information becomes available. Therefore, by definition, everything we know now is wrong. It just happens to be what we know at present, while we wait to make new discoveries.

Characteristics tested by MMI

As indicated above, MMI is purportedly able to detect characteristics desired by professional programs. The test has become a screening tool for personal and professional characteristics, or "non-cognitive" skills and capacities that cannot be deduced by grades and standardized test scores.

In essence, the test claims to identify and evaluate the following in applicants:

1. The ability to make mature decisions under stress.

2. The ability to make ethical and moral choices, given a challenging scenario or ethical dilemma.

3. The capacity to resolve conflicts with peers and superiors.

4. The ability to solve complex problems by considering various perspectives and points of view, while staying objective, rational, and open-minded.

5. The ability to realize team dynamics and become a valuable part of a team.

6. The capacity to fluently communicate thoughts with individuals with varying degrees of knowledge and authority.

In short, the MMI is claimed to test the "soft skills" or people skills of applicants; that is, it examines those qualities and characteristics that are required to practice the "art" of any profession. Thus, it should come as no surprise that your MMI accounts for a significant percentage of your final admissions score and how you perform on this test will determine whether you will be accepted or not.

Now that we have looked at how the MMI started and what characteristics are measured, the following chapter will more thoroughly explore and articulate the test structure and various components involved, before we move onto specific preparation strategies and sample questions.

Chapter II

MMI Structure and Components

How is the MMI structured?

U nlike traditional interviews, where you would be asked questions by the same interviewer(s) in series, MMIs consist of 6 to 12 separate "stations", where you are assessed by independent interviewers. Additionally, there are one or two break stations included for rest, which are important for implementing stress management strategies that we will cover later in *Chapter X: How to Manage Stress.*

The MMI is structured and executed in the following manner: On your interview day, you will rotate through a series of 6 to 12 stations with individuals who may be practicing professionals, faculty members, senior students, administrators, or members of the public. It is also important to note that you can be placed randomly at any of the stations at the start of the process. At each station, you will be provided with a question or a prompt placed on the door of the interview room. You will have a total of 1 to 2 minutes to read the prompt and formulate your response before entering the room. Some schools will provide a pen and paper for you to jot down your thoughts, while other schools will not allow note taking. Similarly, some schools will include a copy of the prompt inside the interview room, while others may not. In this case, if you are not certain about whether you will be able to jot down thoughts during the reflection time, you should prepare for your interview with and without jotting notes, so that you are well-prepared for your actual interview and are not surprised and concerned if you are not provided with pen and paper.

Next, after the 1 to 2 minutes, a buzzer will sound, prompting you to enter the interview room. Depending on the program, you will be given 4 to 8 minutes to discuss your response with the interviewer. If you are finished with your response before the time is up, the interviewer may have follow-up questions. Once the time is up, you will once again hear a buzzer go off, indicating that it is time to leave that interview room and to move on to the next station. This process will repeat until you have completed all of the stations. Most programs will also provide 1 to 2 rest stations to allow you to collect your thoughts and take a deep breath.

Overall, the MMI is a set structure of questions that each applicant receives; the questions are not individualized to the applicant. MMIs are typically "closed book" in the sense that the specifics that you have indicated in your written application are not addressed in the interview and the interviewer has not reviewed your application. Furthermore, the interviewers are "blind" to who you are and what it says in your written application.

Chapter III

How is the MMI Scored?

S imilar to any interview or test, the best way to prepare for it is to understand not only the rationale behind it (which we have already covered in our first chapter), but also how the test is scored.

Who are the MMI interviewers?

Before we go into the grading, let's first look at who rates your interview responses. The interviewers for the MMI are individuals from all walks of life. They may include practicing professionals, professional school students and residents, members of the public, and admissions faculty. Each interviewer receives an overview of the MMI and how it should be scored. Furthermore, the interviewers are provided with questions for the specific station they will be evaluating along with background theory for that station, and are not privy to the other interview questions. The interviewers are also not aware of the applicants' personal identifiers and they do not have access to the applicants' submitted applications. This supposedly helps to increase the inter-observer reliability of the test. The raters are given general information about the concepts important to the station they will be evaluating and the major ideas that should be discussed, but they are not provided with a specific answer key, as there are multiple ways to formulate an appropriate response; similarly, there are many ways to formulate an inappropriate response to complex hypothetical situations presented during the MMI.

How are the interviewers trained?

Each MMI interviewer is provided with a detailed manual on the logistical aspects of marking the MMI, including background information on each assigned station and the criteria they must apply to each response when grading interview responses. Some schools also provide a training session for the interviewers; however, to our knowledge, the interviewers are not rigorously tested to ensure they have a proficient understanding of the process. Yet, this is the aspect of the MMI that is claimed to minimize subjective judgment in favor of objective assessment criteria – notice that we use the term "minimize", not "remove", because answers marked by humans, and even those who are experts in this field will never be 100% objective.

Now you might be thinking, "Wait, so the MMI interviewers are not tested using MMI itself during their training?!" If this question popped in your head, you are already thinking like a true professional and we're glad you are part of the team. To answer your question, based on publicly available information, it does not appear that MMI interviewers are tested using the MMI itself; in fact, as we indicated earlier, they don't seem to be tested on their skills as an interviewer in any rigorous manner. It is odd that the interviewers themselves are not chosen based on their performance on the same interview format, especially if the interview is meant to judge personal and professional characteristics better than anything else. Wouldn't it make sense for a doctor advocating a remedy to take her own medicine?

How is the MMI scored?

MMI responses are graded using a numerical Likert-style scale. The scale runs from 1 to 10, with 1 signifying a "unsuitable" response and 10 signifying an "outstanding" or superior one. The interviewers are instructed to assign a score to each applicant *relative* to all other applicants they have interviewed. Although you may encounter follow-up questions, in addition to the prompt questions, the score that you receive is representative of your *overall* performance on that station. Therefore, it is important to focus on formulating well-thought out answers and having a strategy for every type of MMI prompt (both of which will be discussed shortly), rather than trying to fill the entire allowed response time because you feel pressured to talk the entire time. Remember, the MMI is partly a test of your communications skills, so it is critical that you learn to convey your message in a concise, articulate manner.

According to the publicly available official interviewer manual provided by McMaster (the original creator of the MMI), your responses are assessed based on three criteria at each station: communications skills, strength of argument, and suitability for the profession.

Communication skills:

Communication is critical in any interview, and for the MMI, it is an essential part of your evaluation. You must learn to use concise, formal language and avoid the use of colloquialisms or clichés.

In McMaster's interviewer manual, they define "characteristics of effective communication skills that the applicant might display" in the context of communication-based stations(which we will cover later) as those in which the applicant:

- Listens well

- Remains supportive

- Provides instructee with a sense of the end goal, rather than just leaping into the step-by-step instructions

- Avoids making light of any difficulties experienced by the instructee

- Takes stock of progress, gathering feedback from the instructee and confirming that the project is at the anticipated stage

- Is able to eloquently express instructions and maintain an effective dialogue with instructee during the 3-minute debriefing/feedback session

Strength of arguments

The strength of your arguments is related to the approach you take to tackle each station. You need to showcase a good understanding of the scenario or question posed. This will rest on the rationale you use and the support you provide for each response. In fact, interviewers are asked to challenge applicants on their arguments and evaluate their ability to express their thoughts "clearly and rigorously". This will be discussed further in later chapters, where we will discuss the types of questions you might encounter and which BeMo strategies to utilize for each question type.

Suitability for the profession

Suitability for the profession is essentially a combination of all the traits previously mentioned. These traits are commonly posted on the official website of the regulatory body of each profession. For example, the American Association of Medical Colleges (AAMC) lists specific core competencies that are required by upcoming medical students and future medical doctors. Again, we will go over the essential key traits you must display and how to acquire them in future chapters. Importantly, our strategies will work no matter what professional program you are interviewing for or where the school is located geographically.

Note: Keep in mind that the manual gets updated annually. We recommend that you review the most up-to-date manual and visit the official admissions website for further details.

Comment Section

In addition, there is space for the interviewers to include their commentary. Because each station is scored independently of the others, you are given a fresh approach to each question with a different interviewer. Thus, it is essential to put your best foot forward for each station – regardless of what happened in the previous stations. You do not want your performance on subsequent stations to be compromised by your dissatisfaction with one station; you may struggle with one station but have the capacity to excel at others, but if you carry that disappointment with you, it will be reflected in your performance in other stations. This ability to move on and perform effectively after an upset is a critical quality of a true professional.

What interviewers are not allowed to take into account when scoring your stations:

McMaster's interview manual indicates that interviewers are not allowed to inquire about the following, unless otherwise they are discussed by the applicant *and* they are related to the issue at hand:

- *Age*
- *Ancestry, color, race*
- *Citizenship*
- *Ethnic origin*
- *Place of origin*
- *Creed*
- *Disability*
- *Family status*
- *Marital status*
- *Gender identity, gender expression*
- *Receipt of public assistance*

- *Record of offences*

- *Sex*

- *Sexual orientation*

Will you receive your MMI score?

You will not receive your MMI score and the admissions office usually will not provide you with any form of personalized feedback regarding how to do better if you get rejected.

Now that you understand exactly how the MMI is structured and scored, let's examine its importance to your overall admissions score and chance of acceptance before we jump into specific preparation strategies.

Chapter IV

Admissions Statistics and Why You Must Ace Your MMI

How important is your MMI score? How is it weighted in the overall admissions score? The answer to this question differs for each school. Each school can use your MMI score in any way they see fit in the process of deciding who is admitted and who is rejected. Some universities tell you exactly how they will use your MMI scores, while others aren't as transparent. The best way to find out is to consult the official university admissions website and contact the admissions office for the most up-to-date information. Regardless, your MMI performance is likely going to be a significant factor, if not *the* deciding factor, between an acceptance letter and a rejection letter.

In order to appreciate the importance of the multiple mini interview in the overall admissions process, one particular university provides the best hint at how other schools may be using your MMI score. Recall that MMI was originally introduced by McMaster University, and since then the test has become a for-profit venture. McMaster remains a part-owner of this new company that spreads the use of MMI to other organizations. Given this information, it may be possible to deduce that other schools adopting MMI are most likely following a similar approach to the use of MMI scores in their overall admissions decision.

McMaster medical school receives roughly 5,000 applicants for about 200 spots. This means the success rate is a mere 4%. McMaster also indicates that the MMI accounts for a whopping 70% of the admissions score for each applicant. Next, by looking at McMaster's official admissions statistics for previous years, two very interesting patterns emerge. First, many of applicants with excellent MCAT and GPA scores do *not* gain admission. Second, roughly 30% of accepted applicants have average or below average GPA and MCAT scores, as compared to the average accepted scores!

Thus, regardless of how well you do on your admissions test, and however high your grades may be, without an outstanding multiple mini interview performance, you will not be accepted and your application will likely be rejected. On the other hand, even if you have a below average GPA and admissions test scores, you can still gain admission, if – and only if – you ace your MMI.

This general conclusion can be applied to other schools and programs that are currently utilizing the MMI, as well. Again, the best way to find out is to contact the official admissions office or consult the official admissions statistics. You will notice that almost all schools utilizing MMI accept students who have less than outstanding standardized tests or GPA scores. Therefore, it's clear that you must prepare for and do well on your MMI. There are no shortcuts and no exceptions. If you are still skeptical, ask yourself this: why would a school go to the trouble of using a complicated, time-consuming, and expensive interview format if it was not important?

Chapter V

Top 2 Myths about MMI Preparation They Don't Want You to Know

Before we begin reviewing sample questions, we must first identify the top two myths about how to best prepare for this type of interview. We will then turn our attention to specific preparation strategies, followed by different question types and sample questions and answers in subsequent chapters.

Myth #1: "There are no right or wrong answers."

This is stated on some official admissions websites. This is a complete myth and it is commonly misunderstood by students that get rejected. Notably, although there are no *specific* right or wrong answers when it comes to the various scenarios you encounter on the

MMI, there are appropriate and inappropriate answers that you can provide. If this was not the case, then a lot more individuals with fantastic GPA and standardized test scores would be admitted to any university that use the MMI, but, of course, we now know that this is not the case. Here is another way to think about this myth. If this were true, then everyone would get accepted regardless of their performance on the MMI. The reality is this: there is certainly a difference between a well thought out, mature, professional, and articulate answer and one that is immature, unprofessional, and disorganized. It is your job to learn how to do the former and avoid the latter, otherwise a rejection letter is as likely as the rising sun.

Myth #2: "MMI is immune to coaching", or "You can't prepare in advance."

This is the most common and most absurd myth about the MMI. One that is again, sadly, purported by the MMI creators and mistakenly repeated by some official universities' admissions websites.

Our students do not require convincing, because while we cannot comment on other MMI coaching programs, we know our MMI prep programs work and the results they produce are the reason we have become the global leader in MMI preparation. Notably, our MMI prep programs have an overall success rate of 93.5%. As well, you are clearly not taking such unsupported myths seriously, and that's why you have purchased this book. In fact, most students also joke about this myth and comment on how illogical it sounds. Furthermore, we even have scientific proof to bust this myth, but before we share that with you, let's think about this myth for a moment.

What does the MMI *claim* to test? It claims to test personal and professional characteristics such as empathy, communications skills, and ethics. All these traits are *learned* behaviors. Nobody is *born* with any of these. You either learn these behaviors as part of your upbringing or through deliberate training. Normally, but not always, people from higher socioeconomic status learn to *display* these skills while growing up, largely because of their social environment;

through grooming and specific opportunities for socialization, such candidates have been "preparing" for a test like this for most of their lives, in a sense. This may contribute to their high performance on such interviews. The rest of us must learn how to display these skills actively on our own. When you understand that simple concept, you'll understand how ridiculous it is for someone to claim that it's not possible to prepare for such an interview. You now have an intelligent response whenever someone says something so absurd – whether they are "official" sources or random online forum members, university admissions representatives, or a malicious applicant trying to misguide others in the hopes of gaining a competitive advantage. Myth busted.

If that doesn't convince you, consider this. We recently conducted a double-blind study of our MMI prep program to examine its effectiveness. Double-blind means that neither our students nor our consultants were aware we were conducting the study until after the study completion. This is important because we wanted to avoid confounding factors that could interfere with our study.

The study included 44 applicants with an upcoming multiple mini interview who were selected randomly to participate in the BeMo study. The applicants' baseline performance was determined by conducting a realistic mock MMI (MMI SIM™), using BeMo's MMI Prep program protocols followed by expert feedback and numeric scoring identical to the scoring system used by the official MMI creators. We coached the applicants by identifying areas of improvement and re-tested them using additional independent mock MMIs. Each applicant received a minimum of 6 (and a maximum of 8) mock interviews followed by expert feedback.

The results speak for themselves. Our applicants significantly improved their MMI practice score by 27%, as compared to their baseline performance (and, for those who also participated in our CASPer test study, their CASPer practice score increased by 23%, as compared to their baseline performance). A 27% increase is *huge* when you are competing with thousands and sometimes even tens of thousands of applicants. Even a 1-2% increase could give you an edge in a fierce competition. 27% is the difference between a rejection letter and an acceptance letter. 27% is the difference between disappointment plus thousands of dollars in waste, and enjoying a fulfilling career for the rest of your life. Myth busted again.

Effect of Expert Training on MMI and CASPer Practice Scores

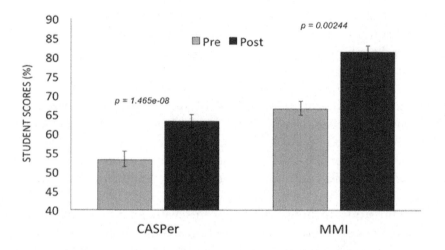

Figure 2. Applicants' MMI practice scores improved by 27% on average after 6-8 MMI preparation sessions and expert feedback with BeMo.

The above two points are sufficient to convince the few applicants who are on the fence or mistakenly guided by the MMI creators' comments. Nevertheless, there are a few other conjunctures that warrant examination here.

They say that some research indicates that practice has no effect on performance.

It is critical to note that in their "research", they did not look at any commercially available preparation program and they certainly did not perform a study of BeMo's MMI prep programs, so it is impossible to make any sort of conclusions. Furthermore, they equate practice with looking over sample questions or going over a sample interview without any feedback.

Well, you see the flaw in this rationale? That's not practice. You don't get practice while you are performing a mock interview. Practice happens way *before* you attend your interview. Furthermore, as we have always said, practice does not make perfect. Practice makes permanent. It is only *perfect* practice that makes perfect. That means you only get better at the MMI if you practice using realistic simulations followed by expert feedback so you can learn from your mistakes. How else are you supposed to get better? You will never magically learn a new skill by mindlessly engaging in the activity. Rather, you need a coach to tell you what you are doing well, and, more importantly, what you are doing poorly and how to do better. You keep doing this until you improve based on the judgment of an expert. Myth busted yet again.

But there's more. Some baselessly state that the performance of students taking preparation programs is likely confounded by the fact that students who use preparation programs are more affluent. Incorrect again. There is clear evidence that interview preparation programs do not contribute to the well-known socioeconomic bias present in professional schools. Instead studies have suggested that it is admissions screening practices themselves, such as the MMI, that are responsible for the bias against applicants from lower income levels.

Two independent studies by SortSmart in the United States and Canada demonstrated that wealth does not correlate with the likelihood of using admissions preparation services. This makes perfect sense. The cost of our services is a fraction of what it costs to obtain a professional degree or attend an in-person multiple mini interview, which often requires applicants to travel thousands of miles and pay thousands of dollars for flights and accommodations, never mind the hefty application costs. Furthermore, professional school students must pay tens of thousands of dollars per year on average just for tuition or risk going into debt and later forced to pay all of it back with interest. Therefore, it's easy to see how naive and false such conjecture appears, even without the facts that show admissions prep does not correlate with wealth.

The two studies by SortSmart, which included a random and representative sample of medical students and residents, had a margin of error of +/-5% and suggested that: admissions appears to favor the wealthy (**Fig. 3**); the wealthy are the most represented group, regardless of admissions screening tool used to select them (**Fig. 4**); 94% of accepted applicants would support a new and improved admissions screening tool (**Fig. 5**); wealth does not correlate with the use of admissions preparation services (**Fig. 6**).

Admissions Favor the Wealthy

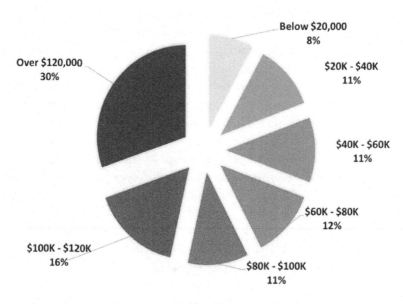

Figure 3. While the median household income in the United States is $60K/year, 69% of medical school students and residents reported household income of over $60k/year at the time of application. Printed by permission from SortSmart Candidate Selection Inc.

Wealthy are Most Represented

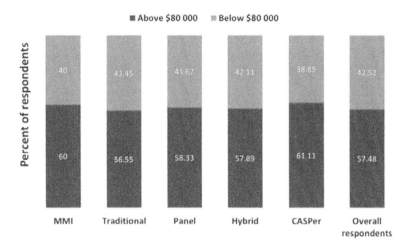

Figure 4. The wealthy are most represented group regardless of admissions tool used to select them. Printed by permission from SortSmart Candidate Selection Inc.

Majority of Future Doctors Support a New Admissions Tool

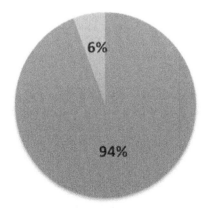

Figure 5. 94% of students and residents would support a new and improved admissions screening tool. Printed with permission from SortSmart Candidate Selection Inc.

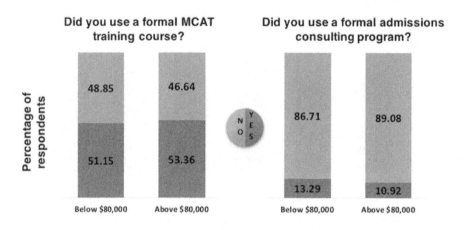

Admissions Prep is not Correlated with Wealth

Did you use a formal MCAT training course?

Did you use a formal admissions consulting program?

Percentage of respondents

48.85   46.64

51.15   53.36

86.71   89.08

13.29   10.92

Below $80,000   Above $80,000

Below $80,000   Above $80,000

Annual household income at the time of application

Figure 6. Wealth Does Not Correlate with the Probability of Use of Admissions Preparation Services.Printed with permission from SortSmart Candidate Selection Inc.

These findings are similar to a report by the New York Medical College (NYMC) that showed underrepresented minority applicants scored lower on CASPer (an online version of MMI), compared to other applicants, and that males scored lower than females, indicating a gender bias. This is corroborated by independent published studies about the Multiple Mini Interview (MMI). MMI has been found to be biased against male applicants and underrepresented minority groups score lower on these types of interviews. You can find the two studies at the following URLs:

https://www.ncbi.nlm.nih.gov/pubmed/28557950

https://www.ncbi.nlm.nih.gov/pubmed/26017355

When you thought it couldn't get any worse, some go even further, claiming (either on "official" sites or on online forums) that they have heard such programs do not help applicants.

Here's another false opinion spread as fact. This type of claim is vague, broad, unverifiable, and unconvincing. How many students using how many different preparation programs did they sample? How do they define "help"? Did it not increase their score at all, or did it not increase as much as they expected? Or did it not help with the butterflies they felt in their bellies the day of the test? With these questions remaining unanswered, such generalizations spread as facts should be viewed with extreme caution. Additionally, online forum users with random names are probably not your most trustworthy sources, and could simply be representatives of admissions offices and administrators, as discussed earlier. Lastly, our success rates and study results speak for themselves. The only waste of money here would be the cost to attend such an interview, plus the cost of reapplication process and loss of time, if you don't prepare well in advance and end up with a rejection letter.

Why do the administrators make such claims? We don't know for sure. This is something you must ask them in a public forum. But here are some plausible explanations, based on our opinion.

It could be that they feel insecure about this interview format, since it has not really been validated as correlating with actual, on-the-job behavior, but rather barely correlates with future test performance. Maybe, that's a point of customer acquisition for them, because promising to new schools that the MMI is better than traditional tools and "immune to preparation" might entice skeptical admissions deans. Maybe they just don't know better. Or, perhaps they simply want to defame us because they don't like the outspoken underdog and advocate for students that has been standing up to them and demanding change.

What we do know is that the administrators do *not* offer any refunds if you get rejected. They do *not* provide any feedback. They do *not* provide you with your MMI scores. They do *not* have any form of satisfaction guarantee. On the other hand, BeMo does offer a bold satisfaction guarantee, because we hold ourselves to a higher standard and we wouldn't create a program that we wouldn't recommend to our own friends and family, at full price.

Furthermore, the reason we exist is to make sure no one is treated unfairly as a result of the current admissions practices, until a fairer and scientific admissions screening process is created and adopted by most universities. In fact, a significant portion of our revenue is used for research and development of a new admissions screening tool. Regardless of what they say, we will continue to advocate for fair and scientific admissions on behalf of all students.

You now have three choices:

1. You can choose to apply to schools that do not require MMI so you don't waste your time and money.

2. You can do absolutely nothing to prepare in advance, like most students who get rejected, and pretend what the "official" sources say is true because it's the easier route.

3. Or, you can reject this utterly nonsensical conjecture about preparation, stand up for yourself, and get ready for your MMI before it's too late.

Ultimately, the choice is yours. Choose wisely.

Chapter VI

Pre-mortem: 18 Proven Strategies to Prepare for and Ace Any MMI Question

A s previously discussed in *Chapter V: Top 2 Myths about MMI Preparation They Don't Want You to Know*, you can and must prepare for MMI in advance. All human behavior is learned behavior and, just like any test, there are specific strategies to prepare and ace your MMI. Our CEO, Dr. Behrouz Moemeni, PhD, was invited to write an article on the Student Doctor Network (SDN) about the MMI. The following is a combination of that original post with additional information. Note that these are the same exact strategies we use in our much sought-after MMI prep programs. They work, and they work consistently. Therefore, take the time to read the following multiple times before you move on to the next chapter, and keep referring to these instructions as you prepare for your actual interview.

What to do during the MMI:

1. Think like the MMI interviewers.

It is important to understand how you are being evaluated before you start preparing for the MMI. McMaster publicly shares the interviewer manual. Importantly, note that interviewers are instructed to rate each response based on three categories, as we discussed earlier:

a) communication skills,

b) the strength of the arguments expressed, and

c) the applicant's suitability for the profession.

In order to think like the interviewer, imagine you are on the other side of the process and you are given the interviewer's manual to rate each applicant. Now, every time you formulate your response, ask yourself whether this fits the criteria in the interviewer's manual, or whether you need to adjust your response to achieve a high score. One of the strategies we use in our MMI prep programs is to teach our students to become MMI experts themselves. We even provide assignments, asking them to create new sample questions as if they were *our* mentors, because the best way to know you have mastered a skill is by being able to teach it to others effectively and effortlessly.

2. Learn to manage your stress.

Nothing is worse than feeling so nervous that you can't even formulate a coherent response when you walk into the interview room. Yet, one of the most common reasons applicants fail their MMI is precisely an inability to control their stress level. Recall that you are being rated on your communications skills, and unless you have your stress levels in check, you won't express yourself articulately.

This point is so important that we have dedicated an entire chapter to long term and short-term strategies for managing stress. Review *Chapter X: How to Manage Stress* to learn more.

3. Read each prompt at least twice.

Make sure you take your time to read each prompt outside of the interview room *at least* twice. If you rush, you are more likely to miss key information and will wind up delivering a poor or even judgmental response. Remember, you usually have 1-2 minutes to read each prompt, then 4-8 minutes to provide a response inside the interview room.

In practice, an organized and concise response should take no longer than 3-4 minutes. This means you'll have extra time inside and can afford an extra minute or two outside the room to make sure you understand the question even after the buzzer sounds. If you do enter the room late, make sure you briefly apologize for the delay, and explain you wanted a bit more time to gather your thoughts before delivering your response. That would actually put you ahead of your competition, because it shows careful thought and deliberation even in high stress situations.

4. Use the "primacy effect" to your advantage.

It goes without saying that once you enter the room, you must smile, say hello, introduce yourself, and when appropriate, even shake hands – all before delivering your response. This is something students often miss: they are too nervous to remember that the MMI is also a test of their professionalism. Interestingly, your interviewer is more likely to remember the first thing you say or do, than anything else that happens after. This is a well-documented phenomenon in psychology, called the "primacy effect", which is the ability to recall earlier events more frequently compared to everything in between in any interaction. In beginning each station by extending a professional courtesy like asking the interviewer's name and using it to greet them, you demonstrate that you understand the importance of such professional courtesies, and – as a result – add a flourish to your performance that will leave you standing out in your interviewer's memory. When you're being evaluated in comparison to all other applicants, little nuances like this can make a significant difference.

5. Master your non-verbal communication skills.

There's ample evidence in the literature that humans more frequently communicate with non-verbal cues and body language than with verbal cues. This includes using eye contact effectively, smiling genuinely, and maintaining a confident body posture.

Eye contact:

As they say, the eye is the window to a person's soul and the eyes don't lie. We are hardwired to recognize eyes because they are a primary mode of communication. For example, infants, who are unable to talk, are able to communicate with their parents with something as simple as eye contact. This is why you may have seen a crying infant going into an almost instant calm after making eye contact with his or her mother. Use your eye contact to distill confidence in the interviewers. You have to practice getting comfortable maintaining eye contact at about 70% of the time without staring. The eye contact says you are paying close attention, you are respectful and not distracted, nervous or on the other extreme threatening.

Facial expressions:

You may have seen some TV shows or movies where FBI agents analyze every aspect of a suspect's facial expression for clues about any deception. While the science of deception detection is still not perfect, there's a great deal of micro-expressions that are used to convey and detect emotions. Again, we are hard-wired to detect happiness, sadness, fear, surprise, disgust, and anger, simply by reading each other's faces. This can also be seen in infants. An angry face usually provokes crying in a baby, whereas a happy face gets the same baby to calm down and smile back. Your goal should be to learn to control your own facial expressions so that you can explicitly show specific emotions when appropriate. For example, if you are in an acting situation and the actor reveals that they just received news that his or her mother passed away from cancer, then you must be able to show genuine concern. Similarly, when you enter the room you need to show that you are excited and happy to be there, instead of anxious, or worse, agitated.

Genuine smile:

You also need to learn the difference between a fake smile and a genuine smile to make sure you are only displaying a genuine, warm smile when appropriate. A genuine smile induces wrinkles around the eyes, whereas a fake one does not, and humans are exceptionally good at distinguishing the two at a subconscious level. If your smile is fake, you may score low because you may appear untrustworthy to the interviewer. If you ensure you're smiling with your mouth and your eyes, you convey the kind of charisma and emotional generosity that draws people in and leaves you standing out in their memory.

Body posture:

Your body posture can say a lot about you, without ever making a sound. In fact, the body seems to have a language of its own, hence the term "body language". Here are a few points to consider when it comes to your body posture during your interview:

When you are interacting with someone – an interviewer, an actor, or another applicant in a collaboration station – make sure you are standing in front of them at a slight angle. Standing behind someone can get their anxiety level up because of the fear of the unknown and standing directly in front of someone may be interpreted as confrontational. As well, if you're standing with someone, be aware of your hands and arms – standing with your hands on your hips can seem aggressive and standing with your arms crossed signifies defensiveness or insecurity.

When you are speaking to anyone you will, of course, be facing them, but in this case, watch your distance. If you are too close, again it may seem intimidating and an invasion of their space; if you are too far, you may seem too distant, aloof, and cold. The optimal space is normally about 1 meter or 3 feet.

If you are sitting down while listening to someone, lean slightly forward to show focus and interest.

6. Identify the most pressing issue.

Your first task is to figure out what the most pressing issue is in the scenario that you are asked to address. Is someone's safety at stake or are there larger implications for the society as a whole? Generally, the most pressing issue in (almost) all MMI stations is the well-being of those under your care.

For example, if you are a doctor, it's the well-being of your patients. If you are a teacher, it's the well-being of your students. If you are the captain of an oil tanker, and the tanker is leaking, the most pressing issue is the well-being of your crew and the immediate and long-term impact of an oil leak on the environment. This is really important, and it comes with practice. Many scenarios will include distracting information or multiple perspectives; while much of this information or many of these perspectives may be important, you must be able to identify and prioritize which is/are the *most* pressing issue/issues.

7. Remain non-judgmental always.

MMI questions are often intentionally missing key information to see if you are going to make a hasty conclusion or if you are going to gather all the facts before making a decision. A professional always reserves judgment until after he or she has all the facts. This brings us to our next tip, and we'll give you an example there.

8. Gather all the facts. Don't make any assumptions.

We just mentioned above that you must remain non-judgmental until you have gathered all the missing facts. Let's assume in an MMI acting station the actor implies that a person is potentially intoxicated and is walking to their car to drive away. How can you be 100% sure they are intoxicated? What if the person has diabetes and what you smell on their breath is ketoacidosis? What if they are indeed drunk, but are simply going to grab something from their car? You don't know until you gather all the facts. Importantly, if gathering facts involves having a sensitive conversation with another individual, make sure you explicitly mention it will be a *private* conversation. As a professional, you never want to have a sensitive conversion and potentially embarrass another person in front of others, unless it is absolutely unavoidable.

Another note regarding assumptions: depending on the intensity of the situation, you may also want to use descriptive terminology to show the evaluator *how* you would act in the situation. In the above example, intervening could possibly provoke an unfriendly response from the supposedly intoxicated person. In that instance, if this was presented in a scenario station (rather than an acting station), you would want to emphasize not only that you would have a private conversation, but that you would approach the individual in a calm, non-confrontational manner and speak with a neutral or friendly tone, to avoid escalating the situation. If you don't tell your interviewer how you would act (or if you don't demonstrate such behaviors in an acting station), then they are free to assume your demeanor in whatever way seems appropriate to them. That's too significant an evaluation to leave unaddressed in an interview meant to evaluate communication skills. Just as you don't want to make assumptions in your response, you also don't want to leave the interviewer to make assumptions about your behavior in a delicate situation.

9. Figure out who is directly or indirectly involved.

As a future professional, you need to show that you understand that real-life situations often impact not only those directly involved in the scenario, but others who are peripherally involved as well. So, let's say you are about to fire the assistant coach of your college basketball team for professional misconduct. Who is directly involved? You, the coach, and the rest of the team. Who is indirectly impacted? The college, the college basketball community at large, the coach's family and so forth. Demonstrating awareness of the complexities of real-life situations indicates a high level of professional consideration and a mature understanding of the repercussions of our actions in the world.

10. Learn to identify and have a strategy for each type of question.

As we mentioned earlier, it's impossible for you to predict what the actual questions are going to be on your real test, but if you learn to identify the different question *types* and have a strategy for each, you'll have a better chance to ace any possible question you face during the test. For example, is the question about solving an ethical dilemma or is it asking your opinion about a specific policy? Is it a case of conflict resolution or does it involve professional boundaries? We have identified 23 possible types of questions and we'll go over each of them in detail in *Chapter VII: 23 Possible Types of MMI Questions*.

11. Provide the most rational and common-sense solution that causes the least amount of harm to those involved, using a simple "if, then" strategy.

Oftentimes, applicants spend a considerable amount of time reading advanced medical ethics books, but that's not necessary and often leads to frustration. The interviewers know that you aren't an ethicist and that you're not yet a practicing professional familiar with all the intricacies of your field. Remember, the MMI is meant to test your professionalism – all you need to do is show that you can make common sense decisions and come up with rational responses that cause as little harm to others as possible. This is best done using a simple "if, then" strategy. For example, "If after gathering all the facts I am convinced that this person is indeed intoxicated, but is grabbing their phone from their car to call a taxi, then I would not interfere, but rather offer help calling a taxi for them. On the other hand, if I am convinced that they are going to drive away intoxicated, then…"

12. Get comfortable with awkward silences.

Remember this is a test of your communications skills more than anything else – after all, that's the hallmark of an excellent future professional. A great professional can convey complex ideas in simple and concise terms. If you are being concise, you are likely to finish your response before the time is up. In fact, we intentionally reduce the interview response time in our mock interviews to just 4 minutes, in order to teach our students to be concise. If the interviewer does not have any follow-up questions, you need to be comfortable with the awkward silence that will ensue until the buzzer sounds. A common mistake students make is to continue rambling until they run out of time, instead of bringing their response to a firm conclusion. As a result, they end up displaying poor communication and time management skills!

13. Don't forget to say your goodbyes!

Remember when we talked about the "primacy effect" earlier? Your second-best friend in the MMI is the "recency effect". The "recency effect", another well-documented principle in psychology, says that people are more likely to remember the last piece of information mentioned than what was said during the body of a conversation or meeting. Therefore, it is critical that you walk out of the interview room leaving a positive impression. It's not rocket science: smile, thank the interviewer for their time, and politely say goodbye before exiting the interview.

Here's what to do when preparing for the MMI:

14. Dedicate at least 6-8 weeks to prepare for the MMI.

Since the MMI is a behavioral type test, you must start preparing well in advance because it takes a long time to develop new habits and get rid of other undesirable behaviors. In our experience it takes at least 6-8 weeks to fully prepare for the MMI.

15. Familiarize yourself with professional ethics.

Some of the MMI stations discuss important concepts related to professional ethics. Therefore, it is important for you to read some general books about professional ethics in your particular field. We don't recommend any specific books, but a Google or Amazon search should give you plenty of options.

16. Avoid overreliance on books and guides.

Books such as this one are a good starting point for preparing for the MMI, but once you have used this book to gain the essential background knowledge, it will be time to put the theory into practice, which brings us to the next point.

17. Practice using realistic mock interviews.

Just like any other functional skill, the only way to improve your MMI performance over time is by deliberately engaging in the task repeatedly. Therefore, simply reading books about MMI or going over sample questions are generally ineffective methods of preparation on their own, unless they are coupled with practicing using realistic and timed simulations. Mock MMIs also remove the element of the "fear of the unknown" and make you less nervous and more confident on the day of the interview.

18. Remember that PERFECT practice makes perfect.

Lastly, it is important to note that only *perfect* practice makes perfect. After all, practicing forms habits, and if you are practicing using inappropriate strategies, you are going to form bad habits, which will impede your ability to do well on this test. Using realistic simulations is great, but it's insufficient without expert feedback. How else will you know whether your responses are full of red flags?

It is critical that you ask an expert – a mature professional, such as a practicing healthcare professional, a medical doctor, a university professor, or anyone with a higher educational background at PhD level – to go over your responses and give you specific feedback on your answers and how to improve. Additionally, this must not be a friend or family member; you want a mock interviewer that won't hold back and who will give honest, critical feedback. This is the most effective way to prepare for MMI. Period.

Alternatively, when you enroll in one of BeMo MMI prep programs, you'll get access to realistic mock interviews followed by expert one-on-one feedback from one of our MMI experts who go over each of your responses, tell you exactly what you did well, what you did poorly, and how to do better so you can learn from your mistakes. To learn more, visit our website at https://bemoacademi-cconsulting.com/mmi-prep.html

BeMo's Proven Strategy to Ace Any MMI Question:

Before we breakdown each question type, we need to talk about the broadest category of questions you are going to encounter during your MMI: the hypothetical or scenario-based questions.

Most scenarios in MMIs are based on hypothetical scenarios that describe a seemingly challenging everyday situation. Therefore, if you have a solid strategy to ace these types of questions, you are well on your way to successfully answering most of the questions on any MMI; if you answer such questions effectively, you are likely to get a higher score than most other applicants. We briefly discussed this strategy in points 6 to 9 in the previous section. Here we expand on these concepts and coalesce them into a comprehensive strategy that you can use to deconstruct and resolve even the most complex scenarios. Remember these are not MMI skills or test skills but life skills that will help you become a better future professional and a better person.

Identify the most pressing issue.

As mentioned earlier, this is the first thing you need to learn to do. You only have a few minutes to deliver your response and if you don't get this part right, you're going to give a response that may seem irrelevant or even dangerous and irresponsible. How do you do this under such time pressure? Well, firstly this will not come naturally for everyone, but it does get easier with practice. One exercise we normally do with our students in our one-on-one MMI prep programs is to ask our students to tell us what they think is the most pressing issue after reading a station prompt. We keep doing this exercise with them until they can consistently identify the most pressing issue.

If you are having a problem identifying the most pressing issue, here's what to do when you read a prompt: find out the consequences of doing absolutely *nothing*. For example, what would happen if someone is indeed drunk and you let them drive? What would happen if you get into a conflict with someone and you do absolutely nothing to resolve it? What would happen if one of your team members refuses to do their part and you do nothing to address that problem? Often, doing this exercise will help point you to the most important issue at hand. It will help you focus before you formulate your response. This will become clear as we go over sample questions in *Chapter XII: 20 Sample Difficult MMI Questions with Expert Answers.*

Reserve judgment until you have all the facts.

Next, you have to gather all of the facts prior to formulating a response. Remember that most MMI questions have a lot of missing information. This is done intentionally to see whether you are going to assume the presence of certain facts that are not explicitly available. Mature professionals reserve judgment until they have all the facts, while being judgmental is often associated with lack of maturity in thinking and in considering multiple perspectives at once.

You should not make any assumptions or hastily jump to any conclusions once you have initially read a prompt. If you approach a scenario judgmentally and form a very quick and superficial decision, then you will provide a response that lacks the nuanced approach that many of these scenarios require. This is a sure way – and the most common way – applicants do poorly on their MMI.

For example, let's say you are working in a group setting and one of the group members complains to you that some other member is not contributing as much. In such a scenario, you are missing a lot of information. What's the definition of adequate contribution? Does each group member have a clear idea of what is expected of them? Is this a one-time occurrence? Is the group member ill or dealing with other extenuating personal matters? Are the two members on good terms with each other, or is there a history of animosity between the two? Clearly, you are missing a lot of information and if you jump to a conclusion and say something like, "Well, in this case I have no choice but to report the slacking group member to our professor", then you have already lost all points for that station because you acted judgmentally without gathering the facts first.

So how do you gather the facts since you are dealing written words on a piece of paper for most stations, except for the acting stations? Simple. You explicitly show the interviewers your thought pattern by verbalizing what you would do in each station. Here's an example: "First, without making a decision, I would have a *private* non-judgmental conversation with the two team members to gather more information." Note the emphasis on the word "private". Whenever your fact-gathering involves speaking to others, make sure you explicitly say that you will have a private conversation – and make this a habit in your own life. This shows that you have emotional and social intelligence and that you don't want to embarrass someone by asking them sensitive questions in public.

The only exception to this rule is when you have to deal with an emergency situation and you don't have the time for a private conversation.

Note that in acting stations, this is actually easier because you can ask the actor(s) questions in real time. Although you have to be prepared for the common uncooperative demeanor of actors. That said, verbalizing the kinds of questions you might ask during your private conversation in a scenario would also be appropriate. For example, following the statement above, we could continue by saying, "During this conversation, I would want to ask each group member to articulate their understanding of the work expected of them, and whether they feel appropriately supported in completing that work. As well, I would want to ask each of them for their sense of how the group is getting along, and whether they, or anyone else in the group, is experiencing extenuating circumstances that may interrupt their portion of the group's work." By showing the interviewer the kinds of queries you would pose in this hypothetical situation, you demonstrate your information-gathering process while also highlighting the maturity of your thought in interrogating complex, and often sensitive, situations.

Determine who is directly and indirectly involved.

As part of your fact-gathering and investigation process, you must also identify all the parties that are directly and indirectly involved in the scenario.

For example, imagine a scenario where you are the physician and you need to communicate a piece of information to a patient. Although, in the scenario there are only 2 individuals directly involved (the doctor and the patient), the delivery of the piece of information to the patient can, at times, also indirectly affect the patient's family, co-workers, the larger medical profession, and/or your fellow physicians and colleagues. For instance, if the news is about a diagnosis regarding a terminal illness, then the information is going to impact the patient and his or her immediate family, friends, and even co-workers. On the other hand, if the same news is delivered hastily without due diligence and it turns out to be a misdiagnosis, now, in addition, the doctor and his or her colleagues, and potentially the entire medical profession, may be involved and impacted as a result. Not only would this be traumatic for the patient, it may lead them to lose faith in the medical establishment, which can have wide-ranging repercussions.

Mature professionals can identify those who will be directly and indirectly impacted by their decisions. Conversely, those who do not have maturity of thought, will not be able to identify the grander implications of their decisions and will only identify those who are directly involved.

Choose the best solution(s) based on sound rational, ethical, legal, and scientific reasoning using "if/then" strategies.

Once you have considered a few practical options or potential possibilities for solutions, choose the one that is the most rational, ethical, legal, scientifically sound decision that causes the least amount of harm to those directly and/or indirectly involved in the scenario. This way you can be sure you have formulated a strong and appropriate response.

In an MMI, you will be asked to explain your thoughts and behaviors around a specific ethical issue. You will have to share your thought process around situations that may reflect a lack of professionalism, crossing professional boundaries, and/or displays of cultural incompetence. Some of these are really complicated. So how do you make the best decision possible, especially when they say "there are no right or wrong answers" – which you now know is a myth?

The best way to formulate your response in a complex situation with a lot of unknowns is by using the "if/then" formula as you verbalize your thought patterns for the raters. This will become clear as we go over several sample questions and provide our expert analysis and response.

Note that the things we have mentioned up to this point have to be done quickly and simultaneously in your mind as you read the prompts. This is precisely why perfect practice is so important – while these things may seem very difficult, if not impossible, to do within such time constraints, these are actually patterns of critical thought that can absolutely be learned and refined over time.

Eventually, you will internalize the process and be able to take these steps quite naturally and in language that is comfortable to you. However, as you initially start practicing, it is a good idea to follow the step-by-step strategy slowly and methodically in order to solidify the process. Once you are comfortable, you should be able to do this process automatically.

Master Strategy from BeMo CEO: See ethical dilemmas everywhere and think like the test creators

To really get these strategies I want you to start seeing ethical dilemmas everywhere. In the ride home from school, in the grocery store, in a classroom setting, in the news, in your favorite show, even in a conversation you had with your mom this morning. Then start applying our strategies to any ethical dilemma you encounter and create an MMI scenario and follow up questions as if you were the test administrator. You know you have truly mastered a skill when you are able to teach the material. One way to become an MMI expert is to create MMI questions daily. Do this simple exercise for 15 minutes a day for the next 30 days and I guarantee you will notice a significant improvement. This will not only help you ace your MMI, but it will help you become a mature professional and a better person, which is the primary goal of this book.

Chapter VII

23 Possible Types of MMI Questions

As we mentioned earlier, one of best way to prepare for the MMI is to learn to identify and have a strategy for each possible type of question, because while there is an infinite possible number of questions, there are finite different *types* of questions.

MMI questions fall into 9 broad categories:

situational/hypothetical or scenario type questions, policy type questions, personal or quirky type questions, acting type questions, drawing/building questions, collaboration type questions, picture-based questions, video-based questions, and writing questions.

Of the 9 broad categories, the situational or scenario type questions are the most common, and most acting stations are a form of a situational question, so that may require very similar strategies, with the only difference being that you will be required to act out your response instead of verbalizing what you would have done.

Furthermore, almost all of the 9 broad categories of questions can fall under 23 different subsets of questions.

Important note: Before we start discussing each of these broad and specific types of MMI questions, note that all schools, regardless of geographical location or program type, use these types of questions to varying degrees. For example, some may use more acting stations while others might use none, and so forth. Importantly, each school can change the question types from one year to another at its sole discretion and without notice to applicants. Therefore, the best strategy is to make sure you are ready for every single type of question regardless of historical trends for a specific school. The last thing you want on your interview date is being bamboozled by questions you have not prepared for in advance when you had a chance to do so. Lastly, it is also possible that you see a brand new question type that's not discussed in this book. That's totally normal and it means that the question is likely a new test question. Furthermore, our goal in this book is not to go over all possible types of questions because that would require us to break down the questions to over 100 different types of questions and that would not be efficient or effective. Rather, we want to teach you the most common types of questions because if you know how to successfully answer at least 80% of questions you are going to be in the 90th percentile of all your peers, and that's sufficient to both help you become a better individual and a successful applicant.

The broad categories of interview questions are:

1. The situational or scenario-based questions

2. The policy type questions

3. The personal or quirky type questions

4. The acting type questions

5. The drawing or building questions

6. The writing questions

7. The collaboration questions

8. The picture-based questions

9. The video-based questions

1. The situational or scenario-based questions

Situational or scenario-based questions are the most commonly encountered type of questions. The prompt will describe a hypothetical situation in which you have been given a specific role. Then, you will be asked to describe how you would react to or deal with the given scenario. The questions can be based on any real-life situation and are not always related specifically to the profession you are pursuing. For example, you can be given a scenario where you are an employee in a bookstore and you have to deal with a disgruntled customer.

The best way to answer these types of questions is by using BeMo's strategy for acing any type of MMI question, which we discussed in the previous chapter. Briefly, the steps require you to identify the most pressing issue while remaining non-judgmental and gathering information, and then formulating an appropriate response using the if/then formula.

2. The policy type questions

Policy type questions will ask for your thoughts on a newly proposed or controversial policy. Any time you are asked about your views or opinions, there are certain steps you should take in order to formulate a positive and appropriate answer. Always avoid stating your opinion on an issue without first considering all sides of the argument. The best way to approach policy type questions is as follows:

First, begin with an introduction: this should be a general statement that shows your awareness of the policy, the complexities surrounding the issue, and why such a policy may be required in the first place. Starting with an introduction will show the interviewer you have a good grasp of the topic being discussed and that you are aware there are multiple sides to the issue. Additionally, referring to any recent news regarding the issue will demonstrate your knowledge of current events. As a future professional in this field, it is important that you begin immersing yourself in the issues that define or challenge that field. Using the introduction to demonstrate at least a general awareness of such issues likewise helps indicate your passion and suitability for the profession.

Once you have introduced your answer and spoken generally about the complexities around the policy at hand, you may begin examining the specific benefits and drawbacks that need to be considered prior to formulating a decision. At this point, you will provide pros and cons from the points of view of those affected by the policy. Keep in mind that you should begin with the positives and negatives from the patient, student, or client's point of view before the positives and negatives for the physician, pharmacist, veterinarian, or other professional. This shows that you consider the well-being of those under your care first, before considering what's best for you.

After you have carefully presented the pros and cons to show that you have the capacity to consider multiple perspectives, you will then, based on the evidence that you have presented, discuss where you stand on the issue.

A common misconception is that the most important part of your response to a policy question is the ultimate decision you make; this is not the case! Instead, what matters most is your ability to demonstrate that you can take a step back and articulate your thought process when analyzing a complex issue. When committing to a final stance on a policy issue, it is a good rule of thumb to side with the option that does the most good and least harm for those under your care or the most vulnerable parties involved. Alternatively, rather than taking a side on the issue, you can provide a unique solution or compromise that would benefit all parties. Keep in mind that if you take this approach, the interviewer may press you to make a decision. If this does happen to you, be prepared to choose one option over another while providing an explanation for your decision. Again, if you have already discussed the complexities of the policy issue and can articulate why you are making that choice, you will do well on your interview regardless of the final decision you make.

In general, when it comes to policy type questions, avoid taking an extreme viewpoint, providing one-sided answers, allowing your emotions to guide your responses, or starting with your own position on the policy. Take a step back and consider the pros and cons for all individuals affected by the policy. And finally, remember that the way you approach the question and discuss your thought process is far more important than your ultimate decision. These issues are controversial for a reason: there are strong arguments to be made for both sides!

3. The personal or "quirky" type questions

Personal, or 'quirky' questions are designed to learn more about you, your past experiences, and the way you handle various situations. You may be asked by the interviewer to "discuss a time when...". The rationale for these types of questions is the belief that the way you behaved in the past is an indicator of how you will behave in the future.

Alternatively, these questions can seem so out of left field that they throw you off pace and out of the flow of the interview. We refer to these types of questions as 'quirky.' Recall that interviews are often designed to see how you react to the unexpected, and quirky questions are one method interviewers use to evaluate your ability to remain calm under stress. Remember that there are often many appropriate answers to a given interview question, and this is especially true of quirky type questions.

Here are some examples of personal and quirky type questions:

1. Describe a time when you came into a conflict with a superior. How did you resolve this conflict?

2. Discuss your greatest limitation with the interviewer. How have you worked to overcome this limitation?

3. Discuss the last book that you read with the interviewer. What were some important lessons that you learned by reading this book that can be used in the future?

4. If you could be any kitchen utensil, what utensil would you be? Discuss this answer with the interviewer.

5. Enter the room and teach the interviewer something unique.

One of the toughest personal questions that most applicants struggle with is: Discuss your motivations for wanting to pursue medicine/dentistry/pharmacy/etc. with the interviewer. Also, discuss why you have selected our program to further your education? This is a very challenging question because it requires you to be sincere and genuine and to be able to thread together your many motivations and experiences into one cohesive response. To speak to the specific program, go to their website to learn a bit about their curriculum, as well as their statement of mission and values, and use these as possible referents for the kinds of skills or qualities you emphasize in answering why you've chosen this particular school/program. It might help to consider what you would say to a friend, classmate, colleague, teammate, or stranger if they asked the same question. If you do not have a clear, concise, and creative narrative that tells them why you have decided to pursue this profession in 30 seconds or less, you will need to do more thinking in order to succeed at this kind of interview station. To answer this question well, you need to be honest with yourself and one hundred percent certain about your intentions to pursue your chosen profession. If you are going to tell the interviewer that you want to help people, you need to think deeper about your motivations. Wanting to help people is a universal drive that evolutionary biology has bestowed on us so that we cooperate as a species to survive. Everybody wants to help somebody, and there are hundreds of different professions that allow you to help people every day. So, why did you choose the specific profession you did? What does this profession uniquely allow you to do that other professions won't? Really take some time to think about this question, so that when you inevitably face this question on your interview trail, you are well-prepared with a polished (but not rehearsed!) answer.

Lastly, probably the most dreaded personal question is "Tell me about yourself". Here the goal is NOT to regurgitate everything you had included in your application, but rather quite the opposite. Instead, you must tell the interviewer who you really are as a person, what you are really passionate about, and how you ended up here.

Crafting this kind of personal narrative requires some introspection, and can actually be a rather fulfilling exercise that helps you learn more about yourself, your motivations, and your goals. Self-reflect well in advance so you have some talking points prior to your interview, but do not memorize your response.

4. The acting station

The next type of station that you may encounter on your interview day is the acting station. At these stations, you will be given a prompt that describes a certain situation and once you enter the room, you are asked to begin acting as if the situation is actually happening. For example, the prompt on the door could read, "Your friend John, who has known you for 10 years, has invited you to his place to discuss a personal matter with you. Walk in and begin talking to your friend John." Essentially, when you enter the room, you will act as if you have just arrived inside your friend's house. How do you normally react when you see a friend or go over to your best friend's house? Act like that!

The prompt may tell you to enter the room and deliver a very difficult piece of information to a patient, colleague, student, or friend. This will require you to truly tune in to the scenario and really act out the emotions that will be involved in those types of scenarios. Remember to always acknowledge the way the other person (i.e., the actor) is feeling, and to take time to listen and empathize. Do not immediately start offering solutions to a problem: first, allow him or her to express his or her emotions and provide reassurance.

Sometimes the acting station will require you to resolve a conflict and to de-escalate a situation that could potentially get heated. The actors may be instructed to be highly uncooperative, and to continuously attempt to escalate the situation. Your job is to remain calm, cool, and collected, and to professionally resolve the situation, even if the actor is insufferable, annoying, impolite, or angering.

In all acting stations, there are two very important things to remember. First, make sure that the words, tone, and body language you use are appropriate for the situation. For example, if a friend shares a piece of good news, it is completely appropriate to smile and tell her how happy you are for her. In contrast, smiling would be inappropriate at any point during an acting station where your friend told you she just lost a loved one. Secondly, always put yourself in the other person's shoes to truly empathize with the way they are feeling and verbalize that empathy. For example, if you have to give someone bad news, it is a good idea to say something like, "I know how difficult this must be for you, and it may seem overwhelming. I will be here to help you through this." Acting does not come naturally to most people, and these stations may feel very uncomfortable at first. It is very difficult to play a role successfully when you're feeling awkward and anxious. To prepare for acting stations, practice delivering both good and bad news in a mirror, ask a friend to role play with you, or sign up for one of BeMo MMI prep programs and pay attention to the acting next time you watch a particularly emotional scene on television or in a movie. With a little thoughtful preparation, you can enter acting stations calm and prepared to successfully navigate any type of situation.

5. The drawing or building station

In a drawing or building station, you will be asked to describe an image to the interviewer or another applicant. The other person will then have to reproduce the image without having seen it. Alternatively, another student may be given the task of describing an image to you.

A variation on this station is to ask you to describe to the interviewer or other applicant how to build or sculpt an object using Lego pieces or clay.

The drawing or building station is used to assess several characteristics: Do you approach problems in an organized and logical manner? Do you possess strong communication skills? Are you able to patiently and clearly translate one form of media (for example, a drawing) into another (for example, verbal instructions)? Are you able to guide a non-specialist listener through a complex task, using language that is accessible to someone unfamiliar with the steps necessary to complete that task?

Before you begin describing the image, take a step back to orient the other person. Make sure they are prepared with a pen and paper and understand the task at hand. Next, give a general overview of the picture or object they are about to draw. For example, you may be given the following sheet of paper:

Rather than immediately describing the black star, begin by orienting the drawer. For example, you might say: "On this sheet of paper, oriented vertically, is a two by two array of four equally spaced black-and-white figures. The array takes up the top half of the page, and each figure measures about 4 inches by 4 inches." Only after you have properly oriented the other person should you ask them to begin drawing. After each step, make sure to pause and ask the interviewer or other applicant if they are following you or if they have any questions. This is very important. You do not want to spend five minutes describing an image in detail only to find that your drawer was lost after your first instruction! This will help you stand out as a candidate who listens while allowing the other person to reproduce the image accurately.

If you are given a simple line drawing or geometric object, we recommend that you use the Cartesian system of x and y coordinates to describe the image to the drawer. To do this, explain to the drawer whether the paper should be oriented horizontally or vertically, and then ask them to draw the axes along the bottom and left side of the page so that the origin of the graph (i.e. point x0 , y0) is at the bottom left corner. Then, ask the person to label equally spaced points on both the X and Y axes from 1 to 10. That way, you know that your scales will be the same, so that the point (5, 5) will correspond to the exact middle of the page both for you and for the drawer.

Once you have oriented the drawer, you will look at your image and decide how many points it must be divided into. For example, if you had to describe a 2 cm by 2 cm square (Note: Choose the most appropriate measurement unit. For example, use inches if you are in interviewing in the United States, but centimeters in you are interviewing in Canada), you would tell the interviewer that the image you would like him or her to reproduce is made up of four points, which you will call A, B, C, and D. Then, you would say, point A on this image is located at x2, y2. Point B is located at x2, y4, and so forth. Then, simply instruct the drawer to connect the appropriate dots together until the exact image is reproduced.

This type of interview station is designed to test your communication skills and problem-solving skills given a highly complex task. Using this approach to help the drawer effectively and systematically reproduce the exact image, in terms of size, direction, orientation, and color, you will make yourself stand out amongst the other candidates. Similar to policy type questions, while the end result is important, bear in mind that the process itself is even more crucial. As a future professional, you will have to make specialist knowledge accessible and comprehensible to non-specialists quite frequently; this kind of station evaluates your ability to use clear, plain language to guide someone else through a complex task. We recommend that you practice reproducing different types of images with friends and family prior to your mock interview and actual interview, so that you are fully aware of the potential difficulties that might arise during this process.

On your interview day, another candidate may be given the task of describing an image to you. As you reproduce the drawing or object, be sure to listen carefully to their instructions and politely ask for clarification, if needed. You may find that you have a difficult time reproducing the image because the other student is not using a very systematic method to describe it to you. If this happens, you may politely interject and suggest that the other student orient you to the bigger picture, or that he or she use the Cartesian system we have just described. Being able to tactfully assist the other applicant will highlight your leadership and teamwork qualities and your capacity to remain calm and composed in a stressful situation, while solving a highly complex task. Displaying these qualities on your interview day will show the admissions committee that you are prepared for a career as a future professional.

6. The writing questions

Most interviews will take the form of a verbal exchange between you and one or more interviewers, but there is another common variation you may encounter and should be prepared for: the writing station. The addition of writing stations in the MMI can work to your advantage. For example, some schools include a 10-minute writing station for three primary reasons: (1) to obtain a writing sample from each applicant, (2) to increase the number of independent scores per applicant, and (3), to increase the number of applicants interviewed without having to increase the number of interviewers. In this case, more students can be interviewed with no additional cost to the university.

The prompt at a writing station will pose a question, but instead of entering the interview room to discuss your response with the interviewer, you will be provided with a pen and paper or, more likely, a computer to write out your answer. Your approach to these types of stations should be no different than the strategies we have discussed. First, start by taking time to carefully consider the question. You should have some idea about the organization and main points of your response before you write your first word because a disorganized essay is much more noticeable than a disorganized verbal response. In addition, remember to leave yourself a bit of time at the end to re-read and edit your response to check for completeness and any grammar or spelling errors. Programs may claim that correct grammar and spelling will not affect your score, but a polished written response is always preferable to a careless one.

7. The collaboration station

The collaboration station can take on many forms: you may be asked to solve a problem or create a plan with another applicant, to teach one another something, to argue opposing sides of an issue, to act out a scenario, or you may simply be asked individual questions while sitting next to one another. In any profession, you will be working as a member of a team, in which each individual is an expert in his or her role and must be able to work effectively with a wide variety of personalities. The key to succeeding in a collaborative interview station is remembering to *collaborate* with the other applicant or applicants so that you all succeed, rather than trying to outshine them. While it may feel as though you are being directly compared with the other interviewee, it is very common for an entire group to perform either very well or very poorly. In fact, the best applicants are the most inclusive, encouraging other interviewees to express their opinions.

8. The picture-based questions

In picture-based stations you will be presented with an abstract picture or a photo representing a social challenge facing our world today and asked to share your thoughts. For example, you may be shown a picture of a mother caring for her child in a war-stricken country in extreme conditions of famine. While these types of questions are rare, you need to be prepared in advance to avoid any fear of the unknown. However, our general strategy to answering these types of questions does not change. Your goal is to succinctly explain your understanding of the social situation – which would only be possible if you have been following current world events – followed by offering any solutions while demonstrating deep empathy without any judgments.

9. The video-based questions

Similar to picture-based questions, video-based questions are also very rare. In these types of stations, you will watch a short video about a social dilemma or a hypothetical situation and asked to explain how you would react. Alternatively, you may see a discussion about a policy and then asked about your opinion. Once again, the best way to answer these questions is to stick to our proven strategies for these types of questions.

Now that we have discussed the 9 broad categories of questions, it time to go over the fine details by discussing each possible type of question that might appear in any station. It is important to note that some questions may relate to more than one question type. For example, you may be asked to describe a time when you were faced with an ethical dilemma, which is both a personal type question, because it asks you to recount a personal experience, as well as a situational-based question, because you are required to explain the thoughts behind your actions in a certain scenario. This will become clear when we review some sample questions later in *Chapter XII*.

23 different types of MMI questions

1. Conflict of interest:

This is rather straightforward. Conflict of interest refers to any scenario where individuals, contrary to their obligation and absolute duty to act for the benefit of those they serve, may be tempted to exploit their relationship or status for their own personal benefit. This happens every time some individual or organization is unable to perform their obligations because of a competing self-serving interest. For example, a hospital director who insists on using products from a company that she receives gifts or compensation from would be said to be in a conflict of interest. A teacher who is assigned to grade test scores of his close friend's son is also in a conflict of interest.

Here are a few really interesting examples for you to think about. A university professor in charge of education research who creates an admissions screening for-profit company from his publicly-funded research is said to be in a conflict of interest because he would not be able to objectively judge new advances in the field if such advances threaten the existence of his newly formed for-profit venture. A university professor who is a director of a for-profit company, such as an admissions screening company, has a conflict of interest if she appears in company related activity – for example, an information webinar for students taking the admissions test -

and introduces herself as professor of the university instead of one of the directors of the company. Similarly, a public university that is tasked with advancing knowledge is said to be in a conflict of interest when its ability to advance discovery is impeded by its interests in a for-profit spin off company. Any of these sound familiar?

2. **Ethical/moral dilemma:**

Ethical dilemmas occur when an individual is faced with a scenario in which any decision taken will lead to some form of moral violation or harm to individuals involved. For example, let's say you are a doctor in an emergency room and you simultaneously receive two patients both requiring a kidney transplant to survive but you only have one kidney available. Or, you witness your best friend stealing from her abusive boss at work who has not paid your friend for the past 2 months. The MMI wants to see evidence that you can make ethically and morally sound decisions even when scenarios appear to be impossible.

3. **Professional boundaries, obligations, and ethics:**

These types of scenarios deal with instances in which effective and appropriate interactions and relationships between the professionals and the public are violated. For instance, a professor having relations with his student outside of the academic setting would be categorized as a violation of professional boundaries.

4. **Scope of practice:**

All professionals are said to have a certain scope of practice. These are laws and regulations that define the procedures, actions, and processes that are permitted for a licensed professional. For example, only medical doctors have it within their scope of practice to prescribe medication. If any other professional prescribes medication, they are said to be acting outside of their scope of practice. Similarly, a physician who has specialized in the neurology cannot advise on the pathologies of the kidney; they would be acting outside of their scope. Likewise, a math teacher is best suited to teach math and not genetics.

5. Social and current events awareness:

Some MMI questions specifically test your awareness of current events and news about the profession. Although these are rare, it is a good idea for you to be aware of all the news and challenges faced by your future profession. The best way to do that is to regularly read the news on the websites of the organization's regulatory body.

6. Autonomy support:

Autonomy support refers to the right of individuals to make decisions about their own well-being without their provider trying to force their own judgments. People's autonomy to think, decide, and act freely must be respected. This is referred to as "patient autonomy" in medicine and it requires the health care provider to educate and inform the patient using the latest scientific evidence so that the patient can make an informed decision. But, importantly, the health care provider is not allowed to make the decision for the patient or force them to choose a treatment, as that would violate the patient's autonomy. Another example is when lawyers provide expert solutions to their clients. Lawyers can only present any possible solutions and their outcomes based on their expertise but cannot make a decision on behalf of their client. The same concept is equally important in other professions and in all circumstances in which the professionals' job is to educate those under their care, based on their expertise in the field, so that care receivers can make sound decisions autonomously. You must apply this mindset in your daily life and on the MMI whenever you are perceived as an expert.

There are only extreme cases when professionals can violate this rule, such as when an individual is found to be not of sound mind or physically incapacitated to an extent that makes him or her unable to communicate and make decisions. In other extreme cases, when someone is likely to cause harm to themselves or others, the ethical obligation to support autonomy is replaced by the ethical, and in some cases legal, obligation to intervene and provide the best care for optimizing health. Therefore, it is important for you to keep good common sense as your best friend in life and for your MMI. There are always exceptions to the principles discussed and you must develop the maturity of thought to exercise good judgment and flexibility when faced with extreme cases.

7. Informed consent:

Another concept related to autonomy support is informed consent. Once you have provided the best possible solutions to those under your care, you have to make sure that they fully understand the solutions and their consequences by answering any and all questions, so that they can make an informed decision. Once care receivers are fully informed, they can give informed consent to either receive or refuse a specific course of action. For example, as a nurse, you must address all questions about a treatment option, or request the help of a doctor to do so when the questions are outside of your scope of practice, so that the patient is truly able to give informed consent to that treatment. An excellent exercise for you to do right now is to think of at least 5 different professions and come up with examples of how autonomy support and informed consent are integral parts of these professions. Then, apply this to 5 different everyday scenarios that involve an expert and a novice or a supervisor and a subordinate.

8. Evidence-based practice:

Practicing professionals are expected to make decisions and provide care and expertise based on scientific evidence, rather than gut feeling or personal opinions. In the absence of scientific evidence, the best source of information is experience accumulated in the profession, such as case studies. Therefore, whether you are a medical doctor, a teacher, a dentist, or a speech therapist, your decisions must be based on sound evidence.

Note that this should be another part of your fact-gathering procedure in complex problems with many unknowns and can be applied to everyday scenarios. This is indeed the point. Remember that an MMI does not test your knowledge of any specific profession; that's something you learn when you get accepted – the interviewers know that you're not yet a practicing professional in the field. However, the test is used to establish whether you understand these fundamental concepts and can successfully apply them to your everyday life before they even consider you as future professional. Therefore, when you communicate your MMI responses, you have to take care to explicitly let the raters know that you are making a certain decision based on evidence.

9. Rural vs. city practice:

As the name implies, this requires you to be aware of the demands and challenges you would face if you were to practice in a rural setting. What are the challenges of working in a rural setting? What are the advantages? Who comes first when considering rural versus city practice, the care provider or the care receiver? Who should decide whether someone ought to practice in the city or a rural area; the care provider? The care receiver? The government? You must know the answer to these very important questions and be able to provide your genuine response if such questions appear during your interview.

10. Legal awareness:

This type of question requires you to be aware of common sense legal vs. illegal procedures. We discussed some of these concepts earlier, such as autonomy support, informed consent, and evidence-based practice. In general, any decision you make must be legally sound in almost all circumstances. We say "almost all" because there may be cases when doing what is legal might cause more harm to those involved. These cases are rarely presented in MMI but are most challenging because they provide a seemingly impossible ethical dilemma for the unprepared applicant and generally for those who lack deep maturity of thought.

While you must always follow the rules of the law, there are times that a legal issue might be outdated and must be reformed and modified by the legal system. In fact, in countries that use the "common law" system, this is precisely how the legal system works. The common law system is practiced by almost one third of all countries around the world, including the United States, the United Kingdom, Canada, Australia and New Zealand. Laws are continuously modified to keep up with the changes in our social environment and advances in technology, science, and general human understanding.

As a disclaimer note that we are not lawyers and we cannot provide any legal advice because it is outside of our "scope of practice" – you see what we just did there? If you want to learn more, you must contact a lawyer. However, note that, in our opinion, MMI is not a test of your deep and detailed legal awareness, but rather common sense, because common law is based on common sense.

11. Alternative solutions:

In almost all professions, there are alternatives to generally accepted practices. For example, in medicine, alternative solutions include those provided by homeopathic medicine, naturopathic medicine, and chiropractic medicine. In teaching, alternative to traditional schooling would be homeschooling or boarding schools. In short, these are scenarios that require you to show awareness of alternative solutions and professions and when and how, if at all, you might recommend such a solution.

12. Non-judgmental approach.

Now, this category is a very special one, because as you recall from our BeMo formula, we talked about how you need to approach all MMI stations from a non-judgmental approach so that you do not jump to any hasty conclusions or take any extreme positions. All scenario-based questions fall under this category in some way, since you should always approach any scenario non-judgmentally and objectively. But note that some MMI stations will specifically present an issue or scenario in a way that would lead unprepared candidates to make a snap judgment, whether this is based on stereotypes, lack of information, or even rhetorical framing. Being non-judgmental at all times requires you to be on the lookout for such things.

Here's an exercise for you to see this in real time. Think about the last 2 important decisions you had to make quickly about a situation or a person. Did you gather all the facts first or did you jump to a conclusion right away? How was your action influenced by your initial rash judgment?

13. Conflict resolution:

This type of scenario, as the name implies, deals with real life scenarios that require you to intervene to resolve a conflict. This can be an internal conflict, a conflict between two individuals unknown to you, or a conflict between you and a superior, a peer, or a colleague. The scenarios will vary in detail, but the essence remains the same. You have to show that you are able to maturely and professionally resolve any conflict and come up with a mutually acceptable solution for all parties involved.

14. Global issues related to the profession:

There may be scenarios that assess your awareness of global issues that might impact your future profession. Once again, the only way to show such knowledge is to continuously read articles, scientific papers, and reports related to your profession from international governing bodies and other reliable sources. After all, if you are truly interested in your future profession, wouldn't it make sense for you to obsess over everything there is to know about it?

15. Cultural sensitivity:

As a future professional you are going to encounter people from different cultural, social, racial, and religious backgrounds. Often, such differences lead to different behaviors, expectations, and beliefs and your job is to show your understanding without any judgment while providing the best care and service possible. For example, what would you do if you were a teacher and a student objected to an exam date due to a religious holiday? Will you come up with a solution to make sure the student is accommodated, while being fair to other students? Or, will you retain a strict exam date?

16. Empathy:

The capacity to understand, to be sensitive to, and to experience the feelings of others, is a critical skill in any profession. When you understand those you serve, you are better able to react and attend to their needs, inquiries, and fears. Importantly, when you are truly empathetic, you can foster a trusting relationship, which in turn promotes better care delivery because when those under your care trust you they are more likely to listen to your recommendations and implement your expert solutions.

17. Confidentiality:

As a professional you have a moral and even legal obligation to keep all information about those under your care confidential at all time. This means you must not reveal the details of any of your conversations or findings about your care receivers to anyone who is not directly involved in providing care for them, including your own close friends and family members. You have to truly understand and display a genuine appreciation that care receivers are revealing very sensitive and sometimes embarrassing information to you as a professional. Therefore, maintaining confidentiality is critical to maintaining a trusting relationship similar to displaying a sense of empathy, as we saw earlier. Just like everything else we have talked about, maintaining confidentiality is critical to your daily life as well.

For example, how would you feel if you found that your best friend revealed your deepest fears to complete strangers, who then used it against you or made fun of you? You would probably never trust your friend with anything sensitive again and will not ask for their help in the future.

18. Beneficence ('do good'):

Beneficence requires that the procedure be provided with the intent of doing good for the care receiver involved or avoiding doing harm.

19. Nonmaleficence ('do no harm'):

Nonmaleficence requires that a procedure does not harm the care receiver involved or others in society. There are different opinions about the concept of harm or doing bad. In healthcare professions, harm is a concept that worsens the condition of the patient. In some cases, it is difficult for health care providers to successfully apply the "do no harm" principle if their morals and beliefs contradict a procedure, such as physician-assisted dying or abortion. We will talk about conscientious objection shortly.

20. Justice:

The concept of justice is most complex. The term "justice" means fairness in treatment. On the other hand, *injustice* means unfairness in treatment and occurs when similar cases do not receive similar treatment. The health care provider must consider four main areas when evaluating justice:

    i.   fair distribution of scarce resources,

    ii. competing needs,

    iii. rights and obligations, and

    iv. potential conflicts with established legislation.

21. Patient-centered:

In a nutshell, being patient-centered means that the healthcare provider puts their patients' needs before their own. To elaborate further, in the introduction to their article, "Ethics, risk, and patient-centered care: How collaboration between clinical ethicists and risk management leads to respectful patient care", Sine and Sharpe clearly state, "patient-centered care is driven in part by the ethical principle of autonomy and considers patients' cultural traditions, personal preferences, values, family situations, and lifestyles". The authors continue to explain that when healthcare providers do not meet patient needs and values, or understand the expectations, the patient may be dissatisfied with their healthcare services. An additional article by Linda Bell entitled, "Patient-Centered Care", stated, "the goal of patient-centered care is to see the patient and family as a single unit. That is, care for the patient includes the family, and decisions made about patient care include the patient's and family's wishes".

22. Conscientious objection:

Conscientious objection relates to there being a sincere objection to participation in an act by reason of moral and ethical beliefs that influence one's views on life. Conscientious objection in medicine is highly relevant to examples such as physician-assisted dying and abortion. A healthcare provider's moral and ethical controversy and disagreement about an act, such as physician-assisted dying and abortion, may prevent the physician from engaging in such act, although it may be legal in your country, state, or province. In the case where conscientious objection comes into play, so does respect for autonomy for physicians. By respecting the autonomy of physicians by understanding that their moral and ethical beliefs are incompatible with following through with an act such as physician-assisted dying and abortion, the physician can recommend other physicians, or the patient may need to seek out other physicians who do not have conscientious objections to such acts.

23. Communication:

Recall that every station is a test of your communication skills. In fact, this is probably the most important skill you must demonstrate, and we intentionally left it for last because it is *that* important; you will be tested on your communications skills on every single question.

How do you demonstrate excellent communications skills? First, think back to some of the tips we provided in the previous chapter. In order to communicate your reasoning, you have to take the time to read each question twice to make sure you fully understand the question and gather your thoughts before you start delivering your response. Second, take care to explicitly explain how you would react in a given scenario because if you miss any details, the interviewers will interpret that as carelessness (remember, they can only evaluate what you tell them and how you convey that information – e.g., they cannot infer empathy if you don't act in an empathetic way and/or give an answer that demonstrates empathetic reasoning). Lastly, have a clear beginning and an end to your response. Help the interviewer understand what you are trying to communicate, and how you reached any conclusions.

The best way to understand these concepts is to see them in action in sample questions and expert answers. In the *Chapter XII*, we're going to go over 20 sample difficult MMI questions. As you go through these sample questions you should write a note beside each question indicating the broad category of question involved. This is a good exercise to get you to think in terms of *types* of questions rather than getting overwhelmed by an infinite number of possible questions.

Chapter VIII

Common Points of Debate in Medicine, Personal Type Questions, and Advanced Preparation Tactics

Familiarize yourself with major points of debate in medicine

Beyond ethical principles, familiarizing yourself with the major points of debate in medicine - or your chosen field - will be valuable to your interview success. Here are a few examples:

- Physician-assisted dying or end-of-life options

- Abortion

- Doctor or pharmacist prescribed birth control

- Vaccination

- Legalization of recreational marijuana or other drugs

- Rural vs. urban healthcare

- Compulsory rural medicine service

- Stem cell research

- Genetic screening

- Prescribing medications to friends and family

- Allocation of finite resources (e.g. choosing which patient receives an organ transplant, which patient should receive the first surgery or the only dialysis machine)

- Prescription pain medication, over-prescription and addiction

- Fee for service vs. salary and other compensation measures

- Obesity epidemic

- Other current issues in the US, Canada, Australia, New Zealand, Israel, the UK, Europe or wherever you are going to have an interview

The list of topics we presented is not exhaustive of all major points of debates in healthcare, however, we provided you with several key major points. By reading the daily news and looking into major points of debate on an ongoing basis, you will acquire the knowledge necessary to address the issues at hand. However, do not underestimate the time you need to spend reading and learning about such topics. This component of preparing for your interview should begin ASAP because crunching in the information at the last minute is not going to be sufficient.

Prepare for personal type questions

When it comes to personal questions, you can predict some common questions that interviewers may ask. So, it is helpful to have these responses premeditated.

- Your biggest accomplishment/proudest moment (academic and/or non-academic)

- Your biggest disappointment/a time you failed

- A time you came into conflict with a peer or a superior and how you resolved this

- An example of overcoming hardship or adversity

- Your biggest strength

- Your biggest weakness

- If you could have any superpower, what would it be?

- And of course, why you want to be a doctor/nurse/pharmacist/veterinarian/etc.

The answers to these questions should be authentic, sincere, and reflective. For example, when answering questions about failure, limitations, or weaknesses, you must be honest in acknowledging the issue, but also demonstrate what you learned or how you've grown as a result of this experience. Don't dwell on the negative. Provide a clear account and then move on the more important part: clearly demonstrating growth, resiliency, and meaningful introspection.

Bonus essential preparation tips

Here are a few final tips to prepare for your interview:

1. It is key to always have questions prepared to ask the interviewers in case they ask you whether you have any questions for them. This is critical because you want to show that you are genuinely interested in attending their specific school and that you have done your research well in advance to know everything there is about the program and school. You may want to know more details about the curriculum, upcoming or recent curricular changes, placements, rates of success for board examinations, research and teaching opportunities, or extra-curricular activities, for example. Being able to ask your questions to the interviewers is an

invaluable opportunity to find out more about the program and school, to demonstrate your enthusiasm for the school's mission and vision, and to highlight the work you've done in exploring the school's offerings to ensure a good organizational fit, so don't miss out on this opportunity and plan ahead.

2. Be prepared to answer follow-up questions about any activity in your application – particularly if you know the interviewer will ask you questions from your application, or if it is an open file interview format. You should be able to speak to each component of your application with ease.

3. Listen to yourself speak all the time. Are you often saying words and phrases such as: "ummm", "like", "so", "because", "just", "honestly", "very", "really", "literally", "stuff", "you know", and "thing"? These words need to be eliminated from your vocabulary as they prevent you from coming across as professional, confident, clear and succinct. We highly recommend that you review *It's the Way You Say It - Second Edition: Becoming Articulate, Well-Spoken, and Clear* by Dr. Carol A. Fleming to learn how to become more articulate, a skill you need for life. We are not personally connected to this book or its author in any way (i.e., there's no conflict of interest in our plugging this book); we just genuinely find it to be one of the best resources out there for improving verbal articulation!

4. Be cognizant about not speaking ill of others. You only want to shed positive light on you, but do not do that by putting others down because that actually sheds negative light on you! Work on being positive and taking a positive approach to others at all times.

5. In addition to always shedding positive light on yourself and others - even if they are your competitors - always finish each question with something positive – whether that is resolution to a conflict, a way that you grew through a difficult experience, or something that will help you in the future. *Never* end a response on a negative note. Recall how we talked about the primacy and recency effect. You do not

want to end your response on a negative note because the last thing you say is what is going to be remembered most by the interviewers.

6. Take full responsibility for all your shortcomings, failures, and weaknesses.

7. When preparing for questions such as "why do you want to be a physician/ /dentist/pharmacist/veterinarian, etc.," or any questions, you not only want to think of specific examples and conjure up a response internally, you want to say your response out loud, audio tape or video tape yourself, listen to what you said, and revise your response. You will be surprised how different it is to think of a response internally and think it is great, and then hear what you say when you verbalize it out loud.

Chapter IX

What to Wear, What to Say, and How to Communicate Non-verbally during Your Interview

Interview Day

The way you present yourself at an interview is much more than the way you respond to the interviewers' questions. This chapter will provide you with information about all of the important things you may not think about when preparing for an interview, including how to dress and present yourself professionally, how to minimize stress, and what to do before and after your interview.

Studies have shown that the first impressions formed within the first few seconds of meeting an interviewer can set the tone for the rest of the interview. Your overall appearance and hygiene are among the first things an interviewer will notice. As such, you should present yourself professionally because you want to be remembered for your friendly personality and strong interview responses, not for your fashion statement! For males, this means wearing a fitted grey, navy, or black suit with a plain white shirt, a simple silk or silk-like tie. This should be paired with coordinating dark-colored dress socks and shoes. Jewelry other than watches and wedding rings should be kept to a minimum. You should be clean-shaven or have neatly-groomed facial hair, and a fresh haircut.

Female candidates should wear a grey, navy blue, or black skirt or pant suit with a white or pastel button-down or pull-over blouse. If you choose to wear a skirt suit, ensure that the skirt comes down to at least the tops of your knees and no more than 2-3 inches above the knee while in a sitting position. Wear neutral-toned stockings and coordinating dark-colored closed-toe shoes that are comfortable. You will likely be walking around a lot on your interview day, and you will not want to be worrying about pain or blisters! Be conservative in your makeup application – aim for a neutral, everyday look, rather than a look fit for a night on the town. Jewelry should be understated and complement your overall look. For example, small stud earrings are more appropriate than large hoops. Your hair may either be worn up or down, as long as it is neat, professional, and does not obscure your face. Some women find it preferable to wear their hair at least partially pulled back to avoid absent-mindedly touching it during the interview.

Both male and female candidates should refrain from using perfume or cologne, as the scent can be distracting and may cause allergic reactions in some sensitive individuals. In fact, several schools specifically request that their applicants not use any strongly scented products for this reason. Also, be aware that body washes and hair products can be strongly scented so be cognizant that although you may not be using perfume or cologne, your other products may be too heavily scented for the purpose of an interview. Before your interview, check your products to see if they are heavily scented, and if so, please use non-scented products for your interview.

The next topic of discussion is about your behavior once you have entered the interview room. Admissions committees understand and appreciate that you will be nervous and act a bit out of character as a result of the stress. This is referred to as the psychometric component of interviews. Remember that there is no need to be nervous about being nervous – in fact, it is expected!

Once inside the room, ensure that you smile and approach your interviewer and offer them your hand to shake. Make sure you have a nice firm grip and you smile and look the interviewer in the eyes as you introduce yourself and say hello. Don't forget to smile. You should be excited to be there and not looking terrified! That's the wrong mental state to be in at that moment. If the interviewer does not provide his or her name, it is appropriate for you to politely ask for the person's name to help engage with the person. Of course, if they inform you that their policies do not allow them to share their names, simply accept the terms with a smile and genuine understanding.

Once the interviewer has introduced him/herself back to you, ensure that you repeat their name so that you can remember it for when the interview is over and you are about to leave the room. For instance, if your interviewer says, "Hello! I'm Dr. Johnson, it is nice to meet you!" You would reply: "Hello Dr. Johnson, it is a pleasure to meet you!" This way you have made a subconscious note of their name. This will come in handy once the interview is over, and you have to leave the room.

Once it is time to leave, it is important that you once again shake your interviewer's hand and thank them for their time. But, you will do it differently from all other candidates, because you have already made a mental note of their name and hopefully used it a few times during your conversation with them. You should say, "Dr. Johnson, it was a pleasure speaking with you, thank you for your time." By simply remembering your interviewers' names and thanking them prior to leaving the room, you will automatically set yourself apart from other candidates because most candidates are so nervous that not only do they not remember the names of their interviewer, but they usually do not say goodbye - they leave the interview room in a state of panic as if the building is on fire. You, however, will be a professional, say your appropriate goodbyes, and walk out cool, calm, and collected.

Let's take a moment to talk about why introductions and goodbyes are critical to your interview performance. We are specifically talking about the primacy and recency effect again, which can greatly influence interviewer's impression of you and your overall interview performance. Recall that, the primacy effect revolves around the concept that information received early in a situation has a disproportionate influence on one's impression of you – regardless of what happens in subsequent situations. Moreover, the initial impressions may endure after your interaction with the interviewer – because of the primacy effect. Research literature that explains this effect discusses the fact that people tend to process and be more attuned to information early on in a conversation, and then fail to process such information later on. Also, at the beginning of an interview for example, the interviewer's short-term memory is not as taxed or cluttered as it is near the end of the interview. So, the person is likely to better recall the information received during the initial segment of the interview. Now, when someone pays equal attention to all information, the primacy effect usually disappears and the recency effect comes into play. Meaning, the person remembers the most recent information best because it is most recent. In the case of an interview, if the interviewer pays equal attention to all of the information, your goodbye will leave a lasting impression on your overall performance. As such, your goodbye is essential to your interview and your overall performance evaluation.

In addition to the primacy and recency effect, it is important to consider the interviewer's mood because mood may influence *how* information is processed. Hendrick and Constantini are two researchers who contributed to understanding the effect of mood on information processing. In short, if an interviewer is in a positive mood, the primacy effect may be magnified. On the other hand, if an interviewer is in a negative mood, the person is likely to pay attention to all information provided, thus, reducing the primacy effect and increasing the recency effect. More recently, a study by Forgas in 2011 titled, "Can negative affect eliminate the power of first impressions? Affective influences on primacy and recency effects in impression formation", provided additional evidence to support the concept that moods can influence the primacy and recency effect. The study provided evidence that the primacy effect can be increased if one is in a positive mood, whereas when one is in a negative mood, the primacy effect can be eliminated and reversed, but the recency effect is accentuated. Interestingly, the recency effect is not heightened because the person is in a negative mood and pays selective attention to the information provided last. Rather, according to Forgas, a negative mood accounts for the absence of the primacy effect in remembering the initial information, and the brain better recalling the most recent information – that being the last information provided.

Overall, whether the primacy or recency effect is heightened, and either the interviewer is in a positive or negative mood, your introduction and/or goodbye will leave a lasting impression. As such, it is vital to your interview success that you take the time to smile and look the interviewer in the eyes as you introduce yourself and say hello. Then, say your appropriate goodbyes, and walk out on a positive, confident note.

Now that we have talked about your hellos and goodbyes, the next tip is in relation to non-verbal communication skills as you engage with an interviewer. First, by non-verbal communication skills, we mean such things as maintaining eye contact with the interviewer as they speak, maintaining eye contact with the panel while you deliver a response, nodding in order to demonstrate your understanding and agreement with someone as they speak, and so on. Essentially, non-verbal communication – including body language – includes all messages conveyed other than words. These messages are key because even before you begin to speak, the interviewer is observing your body gestures and facial expressions. Many people put great emphasis on one's non-verbal communication because non-verbal communication tends to be an unconscious behavior. Moreover, when there is a contradiction between verbal and non-verbal messages, a person will typically believe the non-verbal message more so than the verbal message. For instance, when someone is speaking about being sympathetic or empathetic to a situation, but the tone of voice comes across as uncaring and uninterested, the interviewer will likely regard the response as uncaring and uninterested, rather than sympathetic and empathetic to the situation.

In terms of your interview, once you have said your hellos and introduced yourself, you will most often sit in a chair in front of the interviewer. There is usually a table separating you and the interviewer. Make sure you sit all the way back in your chair, so that your bum is touching the back of the chair. This will ensure that you have very good posture while you are sitting down. Next, make sure your feet are flat on the ground, and that you are not crossing your feet under the table. By crossing your feet, and by taking on such a stress-induced anatomical position, you will begin to send major stress signals to your brain, and in the process alter the physiology of your brain in a negative manner, just like when you see someone having a conversation with his or her arms crossed, or someone who is really jittery and moves around a lot or touches their face too often as they converse. These are all what we like to call "visible signs" of stress. Furthermore, avoid sitting on your hands, having your hands under the table, holding your hands clenched on your own lap, etc. These would also be considered visible signs of stress and by corollary would cause your brain to feel and respond accordingly. You can test this next time you enter a stressful or awkward situation. Pay attention to how you subconsciously take on any or all of these stress postures. Then, pay attention to how your physiology is altered and your heart rate goes up, body temperature increases, and your hands begin to feel clammy. The point is this: your perceptions and thoughts have an impact on your physiology and anatomy, and this rule of thumb goes in the opposite way as well. Your physiology and anatomy impact your thought processes and perceptions. So, pay attention to your body position and non-verbal communication. They can either stress you out or make you relax. Moreover, your body language accounts for up to 90% your overall communication with others and no matter how elegant your words may be, you must also have excellent non-verbal communication to make sure you are not communicating inappropriate messages to your interviewer.

Overall, non-verbal communication is critical to the success of all professionals. Here are a few tips to help improve your non-verbal communication skills

- Maintain eye contact. Rolling your eyes up and around can indicate uncertainty and a lack of confidence. However, you do not want to stare to the point that the interviewers feel they are being interrogated.

- Smile.

- Place both feet flat on the floor and relax your shoulders so they are not raised or flopped to one side.

- Nod your head or say "yes" to show that you are engaging with the person. You do not want to stare blankly at someone as they speak. You need to engage with the interviewer through both words and body language.

- Have a relaxed face in the sense that you are not tensing your eyebrows or squeezing your lips together tightly.

- Pay attention to your tone of voice. You want your voice to project warmth, confidence and interest. You do not want to speak in a monotone voice because the interviewer may lose interest, and you will not come across as engaged, interesting to speak to, or enthusiastic.

Now we are going to provide you with some pointers as to what NOT to do with your non-verbal communication.

- Don't rub or touch your nose, ears, or hair, as this may be interpreted as a sign of dishonesty.

- Do not fidget with your hands, hair, or nails.

- Don't slouch back in your chair, as this posture can make you seem disinterested and unprepared.

- Don't cross your arms while sitting, as it makes you seen upset, defensive, and/or disinterested.

- When shaking the interviewer's hand, do not try to crush their fingers or lightly brush them. Find the balance between being too soft or strong so that you are firm and confident.

- Fidgeting is very distracting for the interviewer. Tapping your heels together or on the floor will make you look awkward, nervous and uncomfortable. Keep your feet flat on the ground.

- Do not laugh and smile when you are unsure or nervous about a situation because it becomes evident to the interviewer that you are nervous or not confident about what you are saying.

Chapter X

How to Manage Stress

One of the most common reasons students fail their interviews is not because they are not good candidates, but rather because during the interview, their nerves get the best of them. They start sweating profusely which shows as embarrassing marks on the armpit area of their shirts and forehead. They have sweaty hands, which is a huge turn off to the receivers of a handshake during the interview. Worse, they stutter upon their own words, have a shaky voice that screams lack of confidence, and cannot find the words to make coherent sentences to showcase their communication skills.

Therefore, it is absolutely critical for you to develop specific strategies to cope with stress. Again, this is a strategy you not only need for your interview but a tool that you can draw upon for the rest of your professional and personal life. In this chapter we're going to teach you both long-term and short-term strategies to manage your stress. Your job is to experiment with all of them and choose the ones that work best for you.

Long-term strategies

Let's begin by first discussing some long-term solutions. First, it goes without saying that the more realistic the mock interviews you do, the more prepared you will be for your actual interview, and, therefore, the more relaxed you will feel. The entire process we have provided and suggested, such as learning the rationale behind an MMI, how it is scored, practicing and having professional feedback from an expert, will make you feel at ease when it comes to your actual interview date.

As part of this long-term stress management strategy, we recommend that prior to your actual interview, you go for a tour of the school to which you have been invited and ask to be taken around the campus by one of the current students. Pay them for their time if you have to motivate them to help you or explore the campus on your own. This process is extremely helpful for a few reasons. First, it will make you more familiar with the entire atmosphere and environment of the place where you will be having your interview, so that when it comes to that actual day, you are not stressed out about not knowing where to go and where to be. Simply knowing where you are going and how to get there will put you at great ease. By visiting the school, you will remove the possibility of being stressed out on your interview day because you are at ease with your environment. We even recommend that you take multiple trips to and from the school to where you will be staying the night before, so you can figure out any traffic patterns and shortcuts. You should even sit down and engage in an enjoyable activity on campus as close to the interview room(s) as possible. This could be having your favorite meal, listening to your favorite music, reading an enjoyable book, or socializing with a friend.

Furthermore, having already spoken to a current student may help you answer some very important questions that may arise during your interview. For example, it is common for interview committees to want to know why you have selected their school, or what you expect to be the most challenging thing you will face while studying at their program. Well, if you have already had a chance to speak to a current student and have been clever enough to pose those questions to them (perhaps not in those exact terms), then you will do better than average when it comes to answering such challenging questions during your interview. Lastly, by mentioning to the interview committee that you have spoken to current students to learn more about the program, you will impress them and show that you are someone who does their due diligence when it comes to making tough life decisions. Having said this, we recommend that you avoid seeking specific interview advice from students because, A) by definition, they are still students and are not at a level to provide mentorship and B) normally, students that get in are not genuinely sure how they did during their interview because the stress of the interview itself leads to short-term memory loss and students are not able to judge their own performance.

Several schools have a day of activities planned that include a tour of the school. These tours may be optional, but it is highly suggested that you go on the optional tours. They provide you the opportunity to view the school, learn about the environment, and possibly meet faculty, staff, and students at the school. This is a great opportunity to build a rapport with those whom you come across. Remember that you are not only interviewing for the program, where representatives of the school decide if you are a good institutional fit, you are also deciding if the school is right for you. While on a tour, you want to gather as much information as possible so that you can better understand whether the program, school, and location of the school is a good fit for you. Considering that you are about to invest several years of your life in the program, you need to be happy with all aspects of the program and external factors beyond academia, such as school environment and access to gymnasium facilities, for example. Remember, you are choosing them as much as they are choosing you and this mind set is very important to remain confident.

Short-term strategies

With that said, let's move on to some stress management strategies that you can draw upon in the days or hours leading up to your interview. The American Institute of Stress highlights that the concept of stress differs from person to person. There are also endless ways to cope with stress ranging from deep breathing, listening to music, exercising, cooking, writing in a daily journal, and playing with pets or watching funny or cute videos of animals.

There are ways to deal with stress in the short run that actually cause more damage in the future. As such, you should *avoid* the following:

- Smoking

- Drinking alcohol

- Bingeing on comfort food that is not healthy

- Withdrawing from friends, family, and hobbies or taking your stress out on friends and family. However, if you have a friend who you know stresses you out, try to limit the time you spend around that person so that more stress is not inflicted on you.

- Sleeping too much or too little.

- Lack of exercise. Any form of physical activity will help to relieve stress and frustration: weight training, running, swimming, or playing a sport. On the other hand, exercising so much that you are avoiding other responsibilities, and having drastic weight loss for example, is not healthy. You need to have a healthy balance for you depending on your current level of activity and health.

- Unhealthy dieting. Increasing your caffeine and sugar intake. Caffeine highs and sugar may temporarily make you feel better, but they often result in mood swings that end with a crash. The last thing you want to do is have your energy crash when you are halfway through your interviews. With proper nutrition, a balanced lifestyle, and healthy amounts of sleep and exercise, you will be at your peak during your interview and put your best foot forward.

Let's move on to some short-term stress management strategies that you can draw upon immediately before your interview. We should start by discussing what you should be doing the night before to reduce your anxiety and stress.

The night before your interview date should <u>not</u> be spent reviewing or preparing for your interview. By then, you should have already prepared yourself and the night before your actual interview should be used to relax, enjoy, practice self-care and decompress. Preparing on the day of, or the night before, can actually have detrimental effects on your performance. Therefore, go to bed early, get a good night's sleep, and wake up bright and early. Make sure you are up early enough to have a good breakfast, get prepared, and have ample time to travel to your destination.

The minute you wake up and open your eyes, begin by having one positive thought and reminding yourself of the great opportunity that is ahead of you today. Reinforce the notion that you are fully confident, and are prepared to face anything today, because you have spent a lot of time doing all of the right things in advance. One positive thought in the morning can transform your whole day. You can even write yourself a positive, affirming note to put on your bedside table or attach such a note to your morning alarm on your phone. Remember, it is all about putting yourself into a positive and confident psychological state – much like a professional athlete who gets into the zone prior to major competition. Psychology is everything.

Also note that, if you are to be at your interview destination at 9 am, we recommend that you plan in such a way that you are there no later than 8:30. You should have mapped out several routes to the interview destination several days in advance, so that you are certain as to how long it will take you to get to your interview, and what you should do in case the primary route of travel is unexpectedly blocked or congested due to traffic.

Prior to your interview, place a clean pen or pencil horizontally into your mouth so that you are gently biting down on the pen or pencil with your back molars. This will cause your facial muscles to be placed into an anatomical position that mimics a big smile. Leave the pen or pencil in your mouth for about 2 minutes, take it out for a few minutes, and then repeat for another 2 minutes. By doing this, you will trick your brain into thinking that you are smiling and laughing, and in the process will begin to release certain neurotransmitters that will actually put you in a better mood and a more positive state of mind. This process actually works more effectively if you do it in front of a mirror, or alternatively, stand in front of the mirror and watch yourself smile. Your brain physiology will change, and you will feel more assertive.

As you are in the passenger seat or backseat on the way to the interview, it is also a good idea to put your seat back, put your hands behind your head, put your feet up on the dash and do some breathing exercises. By leaning back with your hands behind your head and putting your feet up somewhere, you take on a very dominant, assertive, and relaxed anatomical position, and as we have discussed above, this will trick your brain into thinking you are feeling assertive, dominant and relaxed and, in the process, release neurotransmitters that will actually work toward that end.

Here's how to reduce your stress level using breathing exercises. By breathing exercises, we mean taking a deep breath in through your nose for approximately 5-6 seconds, ensuring that you are using your diaphragm so that your belly puffs out, holding that breath for 4 seconds, and then exhaling for a prolonged 7-10 seconds, once again using your diaphragm to push the air out. It should sound like an audible sigh as you breathe out. Repeat this a few times during your drive.

This may sound like something a Buddhist monk might do, and you are right, it is. And there is very good scientific reasoning behind this. The prolonged exhalation causes your parasympathetic nervous system to activate, and simultaneously tones down your sympathetic nervous system. You can actually test this yourself if you have access to a stethoscope. Place the stethoscope over your heart and take a deep breath in through your nose. As you do this notice how your heart rate increases. Then, begin to exhale very slowly as we described earlier, and notice how your heart rate begins to slow down. This is actually how your doctor tests your sympathetic-parasympathetic tone.

Prolonged exhalation is an evolutionary tool that has been left at our disposal to release stress whenever we are feeling overwhelmed. This is the reason every culture in the world has a variation of our own "sigh of relief". When someone takes a deep breath and releases a sigh of relief, they are actually causing prolonged diaphragmatic exhalation, which reduces the sympathetic tone. This is the exact same reason you feel more relaxed after a good laugh, or cry, or a really big yawn. All those activities involve prolonged exhalation and therefore activate your parasympathetic nervous system. This is the reason why professional basketball players take a few deep breaths when they are about to shoot a free throw, or a soccer player takes a few moments to do breathing exercises before taking a penalty kick. In fact, even military snipers are trained to do breathing exercises before taking a shot because it helps to activate the parasympathetic nervous system and reduces their heart rate and breathing rate. So, take advantage of this evolutionary tool and make yourself more relaxed on your way to the interview.

Once you arrive at your destination, keep in mind that your interview starts the minute you walk into the building and not necessarily once you are in the interview room. Remember that you will be greeted by administrative staff, faculty members, students, and so forth once you enter the building, so it is important to look excited to be there, be very polite and pleasant with everyone you meet, and show your interpersonal skills right away. Also, make sure that you interact with the other candidates who are there to be interviewed, rather than sitting in a corner by yourself before your interview starts. That does not do well for your demonstration of strong people skills. Approach the other candidates with respect, say hello, and start to have small talk about where they went to school, what they studied, etc. If you notice someone is really nervous, teach them some of the techniques we showed you in this book. A great professional is always helping others, even their own competitors.

A few minutes before you are to begin the interview, go to the bathroom where there is no one around and stand there for about 30 seconds with your arms stretched out big in the air, your chest out, head up, and with your feet shoulder width apart. This is yet another dominant body position you can take in order to make yourself feel more confident and assertive. Do a few more breathing exercises, and lastly wash your hands with warm water and soap to get any and all clamminess right off. It also helps to have a handkerchief in your pocket for wiping your hand before you enter each interview room. By this time, you should be feeling very relaxed and confident.

Chapter XI

Post-mortem: What to Do AFTER Your Interview

The #1 thing to do after your interview that's missed by 98% of applicants

Before we dive into sample questions we need to pause and talk about something that you should do right after your interview that's often missed by most applicants because once the interview is over, your job is not done yet.

First, make sure that as you walk out of the interview room and eventually out of the campus, you continue to smile and be pleasant to everyone around you, even if you think you just had the worst interview of your life. There's a good chance that you are still being watched by admissions staff and administrators and you want to leave them with a great last impression of you.

Next, instead of calling your friends and family or celebrating, turn off your phone and find a quiet area to self-reflect. Write down everything you remember from the moment you got on the campus to the minute you walked out. Write down all the details about all the interactions you had, the questions you faced, the answers you provided, the verbal and non-verbal cues you received from interviewers and everything in between. You have about 30 minutes to do this before the adrenaline and the stress of the situation starts wiping your short-term memory. This is why detectives force trauma victims to sit down and explain exactly what happened as soon as possible, even if it means asking them to delay grievance, because science has shown that we have a small window of opportunity to recall the details of a stressful situation before our memory is distorted or lost.

This exercise is important because it allows you to learn from your mistakes so that you can do even better in the future. In fact, as a future professional you need to learn to make a habit of conducting a pre-mortem (what might go wrong) and post-mortem (what did go wrong) to continuously refine your skills in any field.

Remember that preparing for your interviews was not meant to teach you "tricks" on how to get in, rather our goal is to help you learn how to communicate effectively. Your interview preparation will be helpful when it comes to residency interviews, academic and job interviews. You are preparing yourself to be able to highlight your critical thinking, communication, self-awareness, patience, perceptiveness, and skills in dealing with difficult or unexpected situations, for example. The goal is to improve yourself overall, not just your interview performance, so you can be the best person and future professional possible.

Should you send a thank-you note?

Lastly, after your interview, you should write a thank-you email to the admissions committee. We do not suggest writing a thank you email to each of your interviewers, but a thank-you letter to the admissions committee is appropriate. The email does not have to be long and drawn out, rather short and to the point about how grateful you are for the opportunity to be considered for admission, and that you are looking forward to learning about your potential future at the school. Beyond a thank-you letter, you do not want to "stalk" the admissions committee. Always follow the instructions provided by the school. If they say acceptances will be given out starting on a specific date, do not call every day beforehand to see if you have been accepted. You also do not want to bombard them with emails about whether you have been accepted; rather, you want to thank them for the opportunity and leave it at that.

Chapter XII

20 Sample Difficult MMI Questions with Expert Responses and Analysis

The following is a list of sample questions similar to those you would find during an MMI. To get the most out of this section, try using these sample questions as a practice exam by generating your own answers, and then comparing them to the provided responses and discussion.

For each station, we have provided two answers, one of which is an example of an excellent answer and another that would likely be red-flagged as a bad or unethical answer. Throughout these answers, in brackets, you will find the various components of the answer noted, which will help you to recognize the framework used for each answer.

Note that the "GOOD" answers were intentionally made longer than what you might be able to deliver during your actual

interview for training purposes. You do not need to state every possible hypothetical to score high; in fact, you should be as concise as possible. But, as your mentors, we want to give you the full range of solutions in as much detail as possible, to best enhance your learning experience.

After going through examples of a good and bad answer, we will then outline the rationale behind answers, focusing on what was good and bad about each response in the discussion section.

As you go through these sample questions, note that almost all scenario-based questions can be turned into acting stations and your approach will be almost identical, except instead of saying what you would do, you would actually have to act it out while displaying appropriate emotions.

Scenario-based Questions

Station #1: Scenario-based Question

You are a university student in a small seminar course run by your newly-appointed academic supervisor. With only 10 students in the course and class time mostly devoted to open discussion, everyone is eager to stand out and impress the professor. One morning, on the third day of class, one of your classmates approaches you. Appearing tired and flustered, she explains that she's been dealing with some personal issues that kept her from completing this week's readings and asks if you can summarize these readings for her, so that she can at least follow along during class. You've already composed such a summary in preparation for today's class discussion, so you gladly sit down with her and share your ideas. At the beginning of class, the professor asks if anyone can start the discussion with a summary of the readings. Ready and waiting, you confidently raise your hand; so does the girl you spoke with before class. The professor calls on her first, and she repeats - verbatim - the summary you gave her earlier. The professor commends her for her careful, nuanced, and sophisticated understanding of the deeply complex text, and beams as she proclaims the summary "perfect". What do you do?

Theme(s): ethical dilemma, non-judgmental approach

BAD: This person has essentially plagiarized by offering my ideas as her own. Since my supervisor is also the professor, I definitely want her to know that such impressive work is actually mine. I would immediately raise my hand again to draw the professor's attention, and when called upon, I would expose my classmate as intellectually dishonest **(lack of maturity, fostering conflict, inappropriate response)**. It is wrong for her to get credit when she didn't do any work, and everyone in the class should be aware of her wrongdoing, so that they can protect their own work, in the event that she approaches any other students for such assistance **(judgmental, assumptions around intention)**. Additionally, I want my supervisor to see that I am dedicated to academic integrity, and that I'm willing to call out those who violate this foundation of scholarly work **(overly prideful, self-centered)**.

GOOD: In this scenario, a classmate has claimed my reading summary as her own, after she approached me before class for help understanding the day's readings, which she had not completed due to a personal emergency. The professor of the course is also my supervisor, and all 10 students in the course are vying for the professor's favor **(recap)**. This is a complicated ethical issue, and while feeling upset about this is a normal reaction, I want to ensure that I'm handling the situation in a way that is mature and appropriate, balancing my own needs with those of my classmate and with those of our broader classroom community **(most pressing issue, identifying affected parties)**. There are two competing issues here: academic integrity and the needs of a fellow student in distress **(problem/value identification)**. In the immediate context of the class, I would refrain from disrupting the conversation or calling out my classmate in front of others. I've put the effort into doing the readings, and there will be plenty of opportunities in the next 2 hours of class time to impress my supervisor and contribute meaningfully to the conversation. I know from the professor's reaction that my summary was top-notch, so that should give me the confidence needed to express further insights or observations during class discussion. At the end of the class, I would attempt to get my classmate's attention and ask if I could speak further with her. I would find a private place for us to speak, and I would address her in a calm, non-confrontational manner (**demonstrating tone and approach**). I would begin by telling her that I sympathize with her situation – surely all students have been in a situation in which urgent personal matters got in the way of completing a course reading, and I'm happy to support my colleagues and to foster an ethic of sharing in academia (**empathy**). I would then express my confusion over her actions in class and ask why she presented my ideas as her own, particularly when she hadn't actually done the reading herself (**information gathering**). I would listen attentively and actively to her explanation. I would remind her that what she did would be considered a violation of academic integrity – plagiarism – and emphasize that her own learning experience is disrupted by not engaging the material herself (**directly and indirectly involved parties – herself, myself, and the broader academic community**). I would request that she consider confessing her actions to the professor; however, for the time being, I would not personally escalate the issue. It's entirely likely that she was simply overwhelmed by the personal issues she's facing and that she was swept up in her desire to impress the professor. So long as this didn't happen again, I would keep this to myself and focus on putting together the best work possible for the course. If, however, I came to learn that she had done something like this again, then I would consider bringing this to the attention of the professor. (**If/then, solutions**)

DISCUSSION: In this scenario, you need to balance your sense of justice and fairness with your empathy for others, while avoiding acting purely on self-interest. In the "BAD" response, the student thinks only of their own self, and makes a bad situation worse for an already struggling and overwhelmed peer. While dedication to academic integrity is laudable, this should be turned into a learning opportunity for the other student, not an opportunity to get ahead by putting someone else down. In the "GOOD" response, the student is empathetic and tries to understand why her colleague has done this. She tries to help her fellow student understand why this behavior is inappropriate and provides room for her to do better in the future. As well, the student recognizes the quality of the work she's put in, and uses this to boost her confidence, rather than doing so by turning her back on a classmate in need.

Station #2: Scenario-based Question

Recently, you had one of your childhood friends stay over for the weekend. You had a blast catching up with your friend. You had the entire weekend planned with site-seeing, dinners, and lots of social gatherings. As you tidy up your place after your friend's visit, you notice that your favorite necklace is missing. As you trace back your steps, you recall your friend admiring your necklace. In fact, you remember as teenagers she once shoplifted at the mall. Your friend calls you while she's on the road thanking you for hosting her, what do you say?

Theme(s): conflict resolution, nonjudgmental approach

BAD: Having known my friend since we were children, and remembering she once shoplifted, it would be very obvious that my friend stole my necklace **(judgmental)**. I would feel completely violated; I cannot believe my friend would steal from me after everything I did for her **(considers only one perspective)**. I would let her know that I found out she took my necklace and I am really upset with her behavior **(quick decision-making, does not gather information)**. I would give her a chance to tell me why she took it. If she apologizes and decides to personally return it back to me, perhaps I will still maintain our friendship. However, I will make sure to never invite her to stay over again **(one-sided solution, insensitive)**.

GOOD: After tidying up from a recent visit from one of my childhood friends, I notice one of my necklaces is missing **(recap)**. I cannot make any assumptions as to where my necklace has gone, and I certainly will not assume that my friend stole the necklace, just because she had admired it or once shoplifted as a teenager

(remains nonjudgmental). I would try to clearly think and trace back my steps to when I last saw it or had it on. I would try to remain calm and look for it in the house **(remains open-minded, investigates).** Perhaps I may have misplaced it or lost it over the weekend. Since my friend did admire my necklace, perhaps she remembers the last time I wore it. I would let my friend know that I misplaced my necklace and ask if she remembers the last time I wore it **(gathers information).** I would need to communicate in a non-judgmental way to ensure I am being respectful towards my friend and not compromising our friendship while still looking for my necklace (**identifies most pressing issue).** Together we can trace back our steps **(collaborating on a solution).** For example, if the last time was the restaurant, I can return to the restaurant and see if my necklace is there. During my conversation with my friend, if I do sense that my friend took it, or she admits she took it, then I would want to know why she did so without asking. Perhaps after she mentioned that she admired it, I may have lent it to her and completely forgot. In the worst-case scenario, if my friend did take my necklace without my permission, I would let her know that her behavior is not acceptable, and it can affect the trust we have **(If/then solutions, presenting the most negative hypothetical last).** Lastly, I would ask her that if she wanted to use or borrow anything of mine to simply ask **(demonstrating respectful and clear communication).** In summary, I would first search for my missing necklace as I could have misplaced it or lent it to my friend. In the case that she did take it, I would respectfully ask her to not take my belonging without my prior knowledge in the future to maintain our trusting relationship **(proactive approach, summary).**

DISCUSSION: In this situation, you are confronted with a difficult situation which suggests that your friend may have stolen something from you. The main concern here is to remain nonjudgmental and, if necessary, be able to communicate such information in a respectful way. In the "BAD" response the candidate jumps quickly to assume that her friend did in fact steal the necklace. The applicant also recalls that, based on one previous incident of shoplifting, her friend must still be the same. Thus, the applicant makes a quick decision to confront the friend and does not consider anyone but their own self.

However, in the "GOOD" response, the individual remains open-minded, and first tries to investigate prior to communicating with the friend. Additionally, the candidate works with the friend to retrace their steps in finding the necklace. In the case the friend may have taken the necklace, the "GOOD" response explores a respectful way to confront the friend, and also presents this worst-case scenario as the last option.

Station #3: Scenario-based Question

You are a nurse at a health care clinic. A patient with epilepsy is scheduled to visit the clinic and the physician, Dr. Singh, assigns you to meet with her. While taking a history from her, she tells you: "I've stopped taking my anti-epileptic medication because it makes me feel drowsy and woozy. Please don't tell Dr. Singh as he'll report me for driving without taking my medicine and my driver's license might get suspended." What would you do in this situation?

Theme(s): patient autonomy, patient confidentiality, ethical dilemma, conflict of interest, scope of practice

BAD: Since I am worried about the patient, I would interrupt the conversation and immediately go and tell Dr. Singh (**not showing empathy to the patient, hasty decision making**). I am just a nurse and I do not want to get in trouble, so I would want Dr. Singh to talk to her in more detail and tell her about the consequences of her actions (**not taking responsibility for patient care, avoiding difficult conversations, not seeing this encounter as a learning experience**). I am not sure what else I could do apart from reporting it to Dr. Singh (**lacks problem-solving approach**).

GOOD: In this situation, I am a nurse seeing a patient with epilepsy who has reported that she is not taking her anti-epileptic medications and does not want me to discuss this with my supervising physician, Dr. Singh (**recap**). My main concern here is ensuring the safety and well-being of my patient, as well as other drivers and pedestrians on the road (**identifies most pressing issue**).

First, I want to speak in more detail to my patient. I do not want to make any assumptions about the information she has just given me until I gather more facts **(remains non-judgmental, gathers information)**. I will gather a full history from her about her symptoms, this medication, when she was prescribed it, and any side effects she has noticed. I will delve into her side effects in detail, asking her when they started and if she has noticed them recently or for a long time. I will also look into her medical history to ensure I understand her full story. I will look up the latest, evidence-based guidelines on how to treat patients with epilepsy, as well as the laws and guidelines in my jurisdiction for patients with epilepsy driving **(looks into many sources of information with an open mind)**. Next, I want to speak to my patient. I will stress to her that her health and safety are paramount and it's important to make sure her epilepsy is treated appropriately while minimizing side effects. I will tell her that, by driving without her epilepsy being managed appropriately, others on the road can also be affected **(emphasizes the main concern to the patient)**. I will also stress the importance of sharing this information with Dr. Singh, as he is my patient's physician and is more experienced than me. Furthermore, I'll emphasize that prescribing any course of action is outside of my expertise and scope of practice. However, to maintain trust with my patient, I will tell her that we can tell Dr. Singh together. She can share her concerns about her current medication and I can support her **(stresses importance of communicating with Dr. Singh, continues to support patient).** I will emphasize that Dr. Singh will also be looking to optimize her health and safety and there are steps that can be taken that don't involve her having her driving privileges taken away. I hope that by having an open and honest discussion with my patient, we will be able to speak to Dr. Singh and formulate a plan for her ongoing treatment and follow-up. On the other hand, if my patient refuses to speak with Dr. Singh, then I will have to tell Dr. Singh myself about the information I have heard from her because of the potential harm to my patient and others on the road **(if-then, solutions)**. I will tell the patient that I must tell Dr. Singh that she is not taking her medications, as her actions can impact her and others' safety and well-being **(informs patient of his or her actions, only breaks patient confidentiality when public is at risk)**. I will then tell Dr. Singh so that we can plan for minimizing the risks to the patient and the general public, whether that means attempting to talk to her again, or reporting to the state or provincial licensing authorities **(actively participates in planning going forward)**. By emphasizing to her the risks of leaving her epilepsy untreated, I hope the patient will work with Dr. Singh and myself to create a new treatment plan; however, if she chooses not to, I will talk to Dr. Singh so we can work towards minimizing the risks to both my patient and the general public **(summary)**.

DISCUSSION: The main issue in this scenario is appreciating the danger to the patient of not having her epilepsy adequately treated, and the risks to public safety of her driving while untreated. Your aim here is to gather information from the patient about why she is choosing not to take the medication and why she is asking you to not tell Dr. Singh. You must interact with the patient in an open and respectful manner, while emphasizing how important it is, both for her and others, to treat her condition in the best possible way. In the BAD answer, the student shows fear by choosing simply to go to Dr. Singh first, without explaining anything to the patient. In the GOOD answer, the student seeks to understand the patient's perspective, explains his or her rationale for the steps he or she is taking, and actively involves the patient in discussing the situation with Dr. Singh. In taking this approach, the student ensures the main concern is addressed while involving the patient and maintaining an open, trust-based relationship with the patient.

Station #4: Scenario-based Question

You are a senior associate at a small law firm, working alone during a busy holiday season. You are tired and stressed about handling all of your cases. A new client, Taylor, is in the waiting room and demanding to see a lawyer today. The front desk informs you that Taylor does not want to see you and is instead insisting on seeing a lawyer of a particular gender; however, the only lawyer that would fit the bill, Jordan, is currently in court with another client. Jordan had told you earlier that this court date would be very important and would have a large impact on the case. How would you handle this situation, and what would you say to Taylor?

Theme(s): conflict resolution, professionalism, ethical dilemma

BAD: I would tell Taylor to leave and come back at another time **(quick to make a decision).** It is not okay for Taylor to ask for a lawyer of a particular gender, because this does not impact the ability of a lawyer to help clients **(judgmental, does not consider multiple perspectives, does not take into account the client's needs).** I do not want to allow this sort of thinking. Also, it would not be right to bother Jordan, especially because it might impact the other client **(one-sided, no solutions proposed).**

GOOD: In this scenario, I am a lawyer working alone at a small firm and I have a client, Taylor, who is requesting to see someone else because of a gender preference. The only lawyer that would meet this request, Jordan, is currently in court with another client. I am asked how I would handle this situation and what I would say to Taylor **(recap).** I need to ensure to act in the best interest of the client while still adhering to my ethical obligation and remaining nondiscriminatory towards the team **(identifies most pressing issue)** First, I would go into the waiting room myself and ask Taylor if it would be okay to speak privately in my office. There, I would ask what Taylor needed help with and, after listening to the answer, would ask if it would be okay for me to help, as I am the only person in the office at the moment. It is possible that the person at the front desk misunderstood and that Taylor does not have a gender preference or is willing to proceed regardless. However, if Taylor did in fact express a gender preference, I would ask if Taylor would be comfortable discussing why. If the reason for the gender preference was not a conscious decision, for example, stemming from a past history of sexual assault, I would apologize for probing and contact Jordan to see whether it might be possible to accommodate Taylor without having an undue impact on the other client. Perhaps I could cover for Jordan in court to mitigate the issue or if that matter is not urgent we can reschedule a meeting between

Taylor and Jordan for another date. If Taylor at any point refused to see me or refused to elaborate, then I would act in the same way because it is possible that Taylor's actions are stemming from a similar reason. On the other hand, Taylor may indicate a preference due to a conscious decision based on long-standing practice, such as cultural or religious reasons **(if/then, solutions)** In this case, I would still try my best to accommodate Taylor, but I would also inquire further about why it was necessary to see a lawyer today and whether another day would be possible without causing undue harm. It is also possible that Taylor is making a conscious decision based on bias, such as believing that female lawyers are less capable **(considers most negative option last)**. If, after discussing all this at length with Taylor, I felt it was very likely that this was the case, I would still offer to help and also suggest the possibility of coming another day. I would also take into account the reasoning for why Taylor wanted to see a lawyer today, which could range from a fear for safety in a domestic violence case to simple intolerance and a feeling of entitlement **(explores multiple perspectives, provides solutions)**. So, on the whole, I would first gather more information from Taylor and then, giving Taylor the benefit of doubt, would try my best to determine the rationale and take that into consideration when deciding upon a response, particularly if there were the potential of impacting another client; in all cases, I would do my best to help **(summary)**.

DISCUSSION: Here, the "BAD" response makes several assumptions and comes to a quick decision, although likely from a desire to do good and avoid condoning intolerance. However, failing to gather further information and neglecting to temper the response are both serious concerns with this response. On the other hand, the "GOOD" response first ascertains the reasoning behind the request and then carefully considers a series of alternatives. In the decision-making, the well-being of the client is clearly the central focus. As a general problem, when it comes to preferences, one must avoid assumptions and assess the underlying reason behind a request. Sometimes, an easy solution is achievable, such as a brief conversation that changes the person's mind. Consider also if another provider is available. However, often one must balance accommodating the request with possible harm to both the requester and/or others. Here, one possible guiding principle is utilitarianism, a simple philosophical view, involving a cost-benefit analysis that determines and pursues the outcome that does the most overall good and/or avoids the most overall harm. This assessment includes both the number of people impacted and the degree of impact. Remember, don't assume the individual is biased and keep in mind the possibility of trauma. Finally, always consider whether you have an obligation to help regardless of how you feel about the other person's reasoning behind the request.

Station #5: Scenario-based Question

Your 21-year-old patient, Miss Parker, was recently diagnosed with thyroid cancer. The cancer is in its early stages and will likely respond very well to conventional treatment. However, Miss Parker states that she is only interested in "natural" remedies. You are worried that if she does not pursue the recommended treatment, the cancer will progress and become life-threatening. You ask Miss Parker if she has spoken with her family regarding the situation, but she states that she has made her own decision and does not want anyone else involved. How would you proceed?

Theme(s): patient autonomy, problem-solving

BAD: I would tell Miss Parker that she is making the wrong choice and emphasize that she needs to agree to the recommended treatment **(ignoring patient autonomy)**. Since she is young, she clearly lacks the knowledge to make the best and most informed decision **(judgmental, inappropriate response)**. I would contact her parents/family to discuss the situation and recruit their help in changing her mind **(red flag, violating patient confidentiality, overstepping professional boundaries)**.

GOOD: In this scenario, Miss Parker has been diagnosed with cancer and is rejecting the recommended conventional therapy which has been shown to be very effective. She is only interested in pursuing natural remedies, and does not want to involve her family in her decision making **(recap)**. I am concerned about the well-being of Miss Parker and whether she is making a fully informed decision, and also if she has an appropriate support system **(identifies most pressing issue)**. I would have a private conversation with Miss Parker to better understand her decision to forego the recommended therapy **(remains non-judgmental, gathers information)**. Perhaps she is concerned about the potential side effects and also about the efficacy of the recommended treatment. I would make sure to educate her fully on the risks, benefits, and alternatives of the treatment that I am recommending, based on scientific research and evidence **(evidence-based practice, ensuring informed consent)**. I would ensure she understands the information I have presented to her. I would collaborate with Miss Parker to try to develop a treatment plan with which she is comfortable, while also emphasizing the high likelihood of success with the treatment I have recommended, as well as the risk of foregoing this treatment. If she is interested in a second opinion, I would refer her to a knowledgeable colleague **(collaboration)**. If, in speaking with Miss Parker, I find that she is struggling emotionally with the diagnosis, I would express my understanding and make sure she knows I am here to support her **(if/then, solutions)**. I would also encourage her to refer to her support system, whether it be family or friends. I would also refer her to support groups and additional counseling services. I want to make sure that Miss Parker's decision not to pursue treatment is not being clouded by her emotional state. I think she would benefit from a strong support system but if Miss Parker does not want to involve her family, then I would have to respect her wishes. Ultimately, if after fully understanding the information I have presented to her, Miss Parker still wishes to only pursue natural remedies, I will have to acknowledge that she has the last say in the matter as long as it is clear that she is of sound mind and age of maturity **(respecting patient autonomy)**.

DISCUSSION: In this scenario, the main issue is that you want to ensure Miss Parker is making a fully informed decision in opting out of the recommended treatment. Your main aim is to understand her hesitation to pursue the recommended therapy and to address any concerns that she has. In the "BAD" answer, the applicant is ignoring patient autonomy by trying to ultimately make the treatment decision for Miss Parker. The "GOOD" response begins with a recap and identifies the pressing issue. It demonstrates the applicant has considered different reasons why Miss Parker wants to forego the recommended treatment and they recognize different approaches and resources they can utilize to work with Miss Parker so ensure she is making an informed decision.

Station #6: Acting Station/Scenario-based Question

You are a college student. You don't have a car, but a classmate and friend of yours, Lauren, recently got a new car. You ask to borrow her car to go buy groceries, as it's very cold outside and you normally need to walk 15 minutes to catch a bus to the grocery store. She is reluctant at first, because this is her new car. However, since you are a close friend of hers, she agrees. As you are driving the car out of Lauren's underground parking garage, you are momentarily distracted by your phone ringing and the front of the car accidentally hits a pillar. The damage is obvious. You stop the car to talk to go and speak to Lauren. Enter the room and discuss how you would approach Lauren.

Theme(s): conflict of interest, conflict resolution, professionalism

Note: Although we have labeled this as an acting station our "BAD" vs. "GOOD" responses are written as if it were a standard question for training purposes. When you practice, try to act out what you would say if this were an acting station.

BAD: I would definitely be scared of telling Lauren **(concerned only about own feelings)**. I would not tell her and just return the car keys **(avoiding difficult discussion)**. If she saw the damage and brought it up to me later, I would probably deny that I damaged the car to avoid unnecessary conflict **(red flag, lack of honesty and integrity)**

GOOD: In this situation, I am a university student who has borrowed her friend's car and caused some damage to it. I need to speak with Lauren about what has happened **(recap)**. My main concern is ensuring that I tell Lauren exactly what happened, and work to rectify the situation **(identifies most pressing issue)**. I understand that this situation is sensitive and that I have inadvertently caused damage to my friend's car. I will be feeling quite nervous about discussing this with Lauren and understand that she may be angry and upset **(sensitivity to self and others)**. I will contact Lauren straight away and arrange to meet with her in person, so I can fully explain what happened. I will make sure I am calm and approach Lauren by telling her exactly what happened. I will emphasize how sorry I am that her new car was damaged. It seems like I got distracted by my phone, but I won't make excuses; rather, I will state that I should not have been distracted by my phone and should have concentrated on driving **(approaches situation calmly, honestly explains, in full detail, what happened)**. I would also want to explain to Lauren that I wish to pay for any damages to the car and that I will take care of everything myself, including arranging a rental car for Lauren while her car is being repaired. Hopefully, I have insurance which can cover this damage, but if I don't, I will need to figure out a way to pay for the damage I caused. Even though my insurance payments may go up, I need to report this accident **(demonstrates high ethical standards)**. If I don't have insurance, I'll find a way to pay for the damages by borrowing money from family and friends or using my credit card because my main concern is to fix Lauren's car without any added inconvenience to her. I would want to let Lauren express how she is feeling to me and understand that she may be upset with me **(empathizes with Lauren)**. I will take her down to the garage to look at her car and be present as she contacts anyone she needs to, such as her insurance company or a family member **(supports his or her friend)**. We may also need to contact the building manager to make sure no damage occurred to the pillar in the parking garage **(proactively takes steps to address all parties influenced by this accident)**. I will make sure to try to keep some contact with Lauren over the next few days, while still giving her the space she needs to process this situation **(supportive but giving Lauren distance)**. I will also make sure to monitor my own driving in the future. I should be aware that I need to concentrate fully and avoid using my phone when I am driving **(if/then, solutions, making necessary changes to own behavior to prevent future incidents)**. I also know that it will take time for Lauren to build her trust in me again and will continue trying to be a supportive friend **(exhibits patience and understands consequences of actions)**. By telling Lauren what happened honestly, reporting this accident to the appropriate authorities, and repairing her car at my own time and expense, I will rectify my mistake, be a supportive friend, and prevent future accidents **(summary)**.

DISCUSSION: In this scenario, the main issue is honestly and promptly telling Lauren about the damage her car has incurred. Your goal here is to both discuss what happened with Lauren and express your contrition; you must also understand that Lauren may be upset or angry with you, and work towards rebuilding her trust in you. This is a very likely case especially in an acting station. In the BAD answer, the candidate shirks his or her responsibility by avoiding the situation. In the GOOD answer, the candidate accepts responsibility, talks to Lauren, and gives her the room to feel upset. The candidate also realizes his or her mistakes and articulates their hopes to prevent these mistakes in the future. To work through this scenario successfully, you should focus on being honest with your friend, acknowledging your mistakes without making excuses, offer to help in any way that you can, and work to prevent mistakes like this from occurring in the future.

Station #7: Scenario-based Question

You are a physician working in an outpatient clinic. A 24-year-old patient comes in stating that they want to stop treating their pain with opioid pain killers because they've read about the harms of opioid addiction. They have requested that they get a prescription for medical marijuana instead. How would you approach this issue?

Theme(s): informed consent, patient autonomy, ethical dilemma

BAD: I would certainly appreciate the patient taking a proactive approach to their health and would commend them for it. Since medical marijuana has become popularized and would be effective, I would agree to the plan for the patient to stop the opioids immediately and give them a prescription for medical marijuana **(hasty decision, does not gather information).** It is probably best for them to not take opioids and medical marijuana is a safe alternative **(lacks maturity of thought, makes a decision using untested assumptions, failure to educate the patient on the pros and cons of each treatment option**).

GOOD: In this scenario, the main concern is ensuring that there is informed consent as my patient has been on chronic opioids and would like to stop. However, they are now requesting a prescription for medical marijuana **(recap).** I need to ensure the well-being of the patient and deliver effective care **(identifies most pressing issue).** I would want to gather more information on the patient's condition, take a full patient history, and do an appropriate physical examination, while also ensuring that I understand the latest research on treating the patient's condition with medical marijuana **(gathering information, taking a patient-centered approach).** I would ask them what their concerns are around opioid use and what they have heard in the media. Depending on the situation, I'd like to let my patient know that it's great that they are motivated to stop using prescription pain killers. Next, I would ensure the patient's information is accurate; if not, I would provide my knowledge on opioids and pain killers. I would also discuss the risks and benefits of medical marijuana with the patient and assess if they are eligible and would benefit from such treatment **(patient education).** After a thorough assessment and physical exam, if I deem that the patient would be appropriate to trial medical marijuana, I would ensure they are fully capable, informed of the risks/benefits/side effects/alternatives, and this decision is voluntary, and then I would either prescribe it to the patient or refer them to a pain specialist for further assessment/prescription if I feel this is outside my scope of practice. Furthermore, if there are other, more appropriate medications/exercise/physiotherapy options, I would offer that as well **(if/then, possible solutions).** As the patient is on their pain journey, I would want to ensure proper follow up, and have the patient book for an appointment in 2-3 weeks to assess their pain management and ensure the risks still outweigh the benefits **(prevention/future planning)**.

DISCUSSION: In this scenario, the main issue is patient safety and informed consent. The patient has presented information they have read/seen in the media and would thus like to switch their pain management regimen. The 'BAD' answer is one that does not take into account how much the patient knows or the accuracy of that information, and assumes the patient is fully aware of the risks/benefits/side effects of both opioids and medical marijuana. In addition, the 'BAD' answer does not fully explore the patient's symptoms – there could be another reason behind their pain or more efficacious treatments that would not be available as there was no further history or physical exam. The 'GOOD' answer takes a balanced approach of gathering information, educating the patient and allowing for informed consent and then providing possible solutions depending on if/then approach.

Station #8: Scenario-based Question

You recently started working at a busy fast food restaurant in a low-income neighborhood. You desperately need the extra cash to pay the bills and you cannot afford to lose this job. One day, you overhear your manager talking to the chef about expired food items, and how "no one will notice". The chef chuckles and replies, "They are all too poor to understand the difference". What will you do?

Theme(s): ethical dilemma, legal awareness, conflict resolution, professionalism

BAD: Although what I heard is concerning, I recently started working at the fast food restaurant, so I would be too afraid to speak up in case I might lose my job **(only considers one's own interest, does not consider impact on others, does not demonstrate conflict resolution)**. Additionally, I trust that if the fast food restaurant has remained busy with items slightly expired, then it does not affect their health or the taste (**does not appear ethical, making decisions based on assumptions**). I would try to stay clear of hearing things I am not supposed to and continue working (**does not propose any solution**).

GOOD: In this scenario, I'm a newly-hired employee at a fast food restaurant. I have overheard a conversation between the chef and the manager, which suggested that expired food may be being served, and which contained disparaging remarks about those in our low-income neighborhood (**recap**). The most pressing issue is the well-being of members of our community (**identifies the most pressing issue**). Although I overheard a concerning conversation between the manager and the chef, I cannot assume anything as I was not a part of the conversation (**remains non-judgmental**). I would definitely want to gather more information, as I may have misheard the conversation or the chef and the manager might have been entertaining a distasteful inside joke. I understand that as a new employee I still have lots to learn, but I feel it would be my professional responsibility to ensure an ethical environment that follows the necessary health and safety policies (**adheres to ethical obligation, considers responsibility over one's interest, has good self-awareness on limitations**). I would first speak with the chef privately and inquire about the kitchen items. If the chef informs me that some items have a long-standing shelf life, I would want to make sure that they are still good to serve. If I do find what the chef tells me to be concerning, then I would follow up with the manager. In a non-judgmental manner, I would approach the manager and inform him that I overheard the conversation and already followed up with the chef to clarify (**ability to communicate difficult conversations**). I would state my concerns about the health and safety regulations, and how that can affect the health of the customers (**considers health consequences on the customers**). Additionally, I would discuss the distasteful comments made towards individuals in the neighborhood. If the manager clarifies that it was a joke, and the items would not be used, then I would encourage the manager to be respectful towards the population they are serving and to not encourage such banter because even if this joke is

117

overheard by others it may damage our reputation. If, however, I believe that the manager and/or the chef continue to act unethically and do not seem remorseful, I will be forced to report this anonymously to the local health inspection agency authorities who will be best suited to investigate immediately. In the meantime, I'll try my best to make sure customers are not served any expired items or that they are aware of such instances **(if/then approach, proposes solutions)**.

DISCUSSION: This scenario-based question presents an ethical concern regarding health and safety regulations. Additionally, as a new employee, it presents a conflict resolution, as you navigate through a difficult conversation with a superior. The pressing concern is to ensure the well-being of the customers while upholding health and safety protocols. In the "BAD" response, the candidate assumes the worst case, but does nothing. The individual only considers their own self as they address the risk it might pose to their position, and not addressing the negative impact it can have on the health of the customers. This differs greatly from the "GOOD" response, as the individual understands the themes and addresses the pressing issue. The candidate gathers information in a non-judgmental way. Additionally, the candidate is able to showcase their conflict resolution skills by taking the concern to the manager and presenting the information tactfully. Furthermore, the candidate is not afraid to report this to the health inspection agency, even if it may cause conflict with superiors at work. Note in this type of scenario, you might be asked a follow up question by an interviewer asking to identify your strategy if the manager threatens to fire you. In such a difficult situation, you will be expected to indicate that health of others is more important than keeping your job. Further, you can add that employment standards do not allow any employer to fire an employee due to voicing legitimate concerns for health and well-being of others. The candidate demonstrates effective communication skills and proposes possible solutions throughout.

Station #9: Scenario-based Question

You are a resident physician and have found today to be a particularly busy day at the hospital. You feel that there are more patients than usual, especially since you are under-staffed today, due to inclement weather and subsequent traffic. Your afternoon starts off with a patient who presents with complicated, atypical symptoms, and the attending physician is still stuck in traffic, instructing all hands to be on deck with this patient, as the attending makes their way to the hospital. The patient's team is comprised of you and two other senior resident physicians. You are in the process of presenting the case to the team and the patient's family, when the attending physician finally walks into the room, and pleasantly greets everyone. You notice that the patient and their respective family members have grown fidgety, uncomfortable, and have become increasingly side-tracked and sullen. Any following questions posed by the attending physician were evaded, and responses were directed to the residents on the opposing side of the room. As the team exits the room, one of the family members takes you to the side and asks that the attending physician not be allowed back into the room during the next follow-up visit, and that it would be best if a "replacement physician" could be found. They explain they would prefer to receive care from a physician that is not of a multicultural background instead. You are now tasked with mediating this situation. How do you go about doing so?

Theme(s): Conflict resolution, professionalism

BAD: I would personally approach the patient and their respective family members and assure them that I will do everything in my power to ensure that a replacement physician will be found upon the next follow-up visit later in the day (**hasty decision, does not fully gather information, disregard for colleague**). Ultimately, every individual is entitled to their opinion, and, as physicians, we should do all that we can to ensure their comfort. It is not my place to try to reason with the patient or question their request, opinions. or comfort level (**does not exercise conflict resolution strategies, presents a one-sided approach, contributes to discriminatory behavior**).

GOOD: In the presented scenario, I observed early on that the patient and their respective family members quickly resort to dismissiveness upon the arrival of the attending physician. This inherently hinders the degree of communication between the patient and the medical team. Furthermore, I am asked to find a replacement surgeon to take over the patient's case, as the patient and their family are refusing to be under the care of a physician that they consider to be of a multicultural background **(recap)**. In this situation, the request of the family member appears to indicate that the patient and family are demonstrating an inherent degree of racial bias against this physician. However, I want to make sure that I'm not making any assumptions and make sure that the patient or the family have not had legitimate previous negative encounters with the physician. In any event, my main priority is to ensure the best care for the patient **(identifies most pressing issue)**. I would first acknowledge that I have heard the patient's concerns and proceed to ask why they would be more comfortable seeking the care of another physician given that the physician is perfectly suited and has the expertise to care for the patient. Next, I would attempt to assure the patient that, as clinicians, our sole priority is to do all that is in our power to ensure that the patient's outcomes are resoundingly positive, and that no physician would compromise or jeopardize that responsibility. I would then ask the patient if they would feel more comfortable having an opportunity to sit down with the physician so as to ask any pertinent questions that would aid in solidifying their comfort with the physician's care plan, as well as with the physician as a person, as you can only begin to imagine the fear and uneasiness that may accompany the patient's current medical circumstance **(patient education, ability to have difficult conversations)**. I would commit to doing all that I can to serve as the liaison between the patient, family, and lead case physician, in the hopes of mediating effective communication to help clear up any judgment, preconceived notions, uneasiness, fear, and stigma surrounding the situation at hand. However, if all my efforts fail, the decision is ultimately for the family to determine who their physician will be **(if/then, solutions)**.

DISCUSSION: In this scenario, the main issue is providing the best care possible to the patient while addressing the potentially discriminatory stance that the family is having towards the attending physician. Your aim as you work through the question is to figure out the reasoning behind the family's discomfort and provide best possible care. In the "BAD" answer, the applicant makes a hasty decision without first gathering more information. There may be many reasons behind their decision and having a clear understanding of what that may be helps address the underlying issue. Perhaps this family had a bad experience with this same physician in the past where they did not see eye-to-eye. Perhaps this specific physician made them feel dismissed or otherwise uncomfortable. Alternatively, they might have had a bad experience with a physician with the same racial background. Ultimately, a discussion around the reasons must ensue with the family and you must aim to either empathize and reassure them or mediate the physician change with your staff. One must be tactful, with excellent communication skills when handling such a conflict. In the "GOOD" answer, a recap is provided and, while a patient-centered approach is still followed, there is an exploration of the problem to help identify a solution using our if/then strategy. Indeed, if it turns out that the family had a negative experience with this specific physician, engaging in such inquiry is also part of that patient-centered care.

Station #10: Scenario-based Question

You are hosting a small party with friends. You learn that Blake, a friend of a friend, is a vegetarian, so you point out the foods that will be okay to eat, including a batch of homemade sugar cookies, based on a recipe that has been in the family for generations. As the party nears its end, Blake approaches you and specifically compliments you on your fantastic sugar cookies. You thank Blake and agree to send the recipe later by email. However, later that night, you realize that the recipe calls for lard, which is fat derived from animals, usually pigs. You feel awful and wonder if it might be kinder to simply omit the lard from the recipe and not mention it to Blake, preventing any feelings of guilt, especially since this was your fault.

How would you handle this situation, and what would you say to Blake?

Theme(s): non-judgmental approach, conflict resolution

BAD: At this point, I can't change the fact that Blake has already eaten the lard and there's no point in mentioning it and causing guilty feelings **(does not take accountability, lacks maturity).** A white lie is the kindest thing to do here. Also, I would remove the lard from the recipe and replace it with vegetable shortening to keep up appearances **(dishonest, insensitive to others, does not explore consequences).** Also, since Blake is a friend of a friend, I would not want Blake to be upset with me or to say bad things about me to our mutual friends **(poor communication skills, driven by selfish interests).**

GOOD: In this scenario, I have hosted a party and accidentally recommended my homemade sugar cookies, which contain animal products, to Blake, a vegetarian attending the party. Blake likes the cookies and asks for the recipe. I am asked how I would handle this situation and what I would say to Blake **(recap).** First, I would try to confirm if Blake is indeed a vegetarian since it seems like I may have learned this second-hand. I would call Blake and confirm that it is an appropriate time to talk. After asking how Blake is doing, I would mention that I have a concern regarding the party and then ask whether it was true that Blake is a vegetarian **(gathering information).** It is possible that my friend was simply mistaken in which case there's not cause for concern and continued discussion. On the other hand, it is possible that Blake is a vegetarian, the reasons for which could range from personal conviction to religious principles to medical dietary restrictions. However, regardless of the reason, if that's the case, I would tell Blake that I made a mistake when I mentioned that the cookies would be okay to eat, and I would apologize profusely for doing so **(if/then, solution, displaying sensitivity and open communication).** I would explain what happened, including the specific reason for the mistake, perhaps stemming from my lack of familiarity with lard. It is possible that

Blake is not particularly disturbed by the news, perhaps not always strictly adhering to a vegetarian diet. On the other hand, it is also possible that Blake may become upset. In this case, I would continue to apologize and ask if there were anything I could do, recognizing that I may not be able to make up for my mistake. I would attempt to comfort Blake; for example, if dietary restrictions were due to religious reasons, I would mention the importance of considering intent and highlight that Blake was ignorant of the content of the cookies despite due diligence done by asking me to clarify. I would also explain that I am still willing to send the recipe but that it would be necessary for Blake to substitute vegetable shortening for the lard. Finally, I would discuss the steps I would take to prevent this sort of mistake in the future, including double-checking ingredients before offering any dietary suggestions. My decision to continue pursuing the conversation would depend on whether or not I felt that I was being successful in making Blake feel better. Although I understand that Blake may avoid feeling upset if not told the truth, I believe it would be worse to lie, even if it were a lie of omission. I believe that Blake has the right to the truth and that, in this case, failing to disclose the truth would more likely result in preventing an uncomfortable situation for myself rather than avoiding harm to Blake. Furthermore, if there's a dietary medical concern, it is my responsibility to let Blake know immediately. (**most pressing issue**)

However, if I were absolutely sure that Blake would come to serious harm based on this knowledge, for example, if religious practices dictated a painful punishment regardless of intent or ignorance, then I would consider withholding the information and, after discussing with an authority figure in the same religion as Blake (**gathering information from a more knowledgeable source**), I might decide not to disclose. However, I would still take steps to prevent this mistake in the future (**if/then, solutions, future planning**).

DISCUSSION: Here, the "BAD" response, at least on the surface, stems from a desire to avoid harm. However, the conclusions are reached quickly without careful consideration and there are several actions suggested that would be misleading, at best. It also lacks a sense of accountability for one's actions and is insensitive to Blake's dietary restrictions. Moreover, the response does not consider the implications of a medical dietary issue which may cause significant harm. The "GOOD" response first ascertains the reasoning and frame of mind of the other person. The error is promptly disclosed, and an apology is quickly forthcoming. Although no obvious "solution" exists, the conversation on the phone, along with the explanations, help mitigate the harm while nonetheless adhering to the truth. In general, when an error is suspected, one must carefully gather information surrounding the event. Although difficult, prompt disclosure of an error, accompanied by an apology is most often the appropriate course of action. Usually, most people prefer to know about a mistake that has caused them harm or potential harm, even if the knowledge itself is painful in some way. Being completely forthcoming about the nature of the error, accepting responsibility, and sincerely apologizing often leads to the best outcomes for both parties. That is, forgiveness is less likely if an error is disclosed after an unnecessary delay or in an evasive manner that does not accept responsibility.

Station #11: Scenario-based Question

You are a physician with a patient named Mariam, who is seeking a medically-assisted death, which has recently become legal in your jurisdiction. Mariam has been diagnosed with Amyotrophic Lateral Sclerosis (also known as ALS, or Lou Gehrig's disease) and has qualified for the procedure. Mariam does not want to end her life immediately as the disease has not progressed to the point of being unbearable; however, she knows it is inevitable. She is concerned, however, with being able to consent in the moment of receiving the procedure, as ALS will impair her cognitive functioning. Currently, the law states that the patient must be able to provide consent right up to the final moment of life, otherwise the procedure would be considered illegal. Knowing this, Mariam is considering ending her life earlier than she would have liked for fear of not being able to end her life when the disease fully takes over her body and having to endure the suffering that comes along with it. As her physician, what would you advise Mariam to do? What are your views on this policy?

Theme(s): patient autonomy, informed consent, medical-legal, ethical/moral dilemma

BAD: I would just tell Mariam to take her chances and see how long she can hold off **(insensitive, quick to make decision)**. I think Mariam shouldn't be ending her life prematurely if she doesn't have to; she is not considering how this might affect her family if she ends her life early **(judgmental)**. I would advise against this request **(does not consider patient autonomy)**.

GOOD: This question addresses the recently-legalized procedure of medically-assisted end-of-life treatment in a particular jurisdiction. However, one of the issues that has arisen with the law is the requirement of consent right up to the moment before the procedure is administered **(recap)**. Although this provision was implemented with good intention as a safeguard and to respect patient autonomy, unfortunately, it has had a negative effect on patients who are suffering with progressive diseases that may leave them incapable of providing consent right before the procedure. Currently, the law is being challenged and the proposed solution to this would be to allow patients to sign a legal document providing advanced consent to receive the treatment when their condition has deteriorated to a certain point; however, this currently is not legal and also raises challenges with regard to subjective evaluations in determining when a disease has reached a certain stage **(pros and cons)**. As her physician, my main concern is the well-being and quality of life of my patient **(most pressing issue)**. I would have a conversation with Mariam and her family about the options. I would want to know when she was diagnosed and how long she has had the disease, the rate of deterioration to this point, and the estimated time she may have left **(collaboration, gathering information)**. I would consult the literature and look at the general trends for people living with ALS from the time of diagnosis to the time of death and the rate of decline in between **(using resources and**

conducting further research). Weighing this against Mariam's current situation, I would inform her of all the available evidence and timelines and discuss her options, keeping in mind that no two patients will respond exactly the same **(if/then, solutions).** I would also let Mariam know that she can appoint a family member to act on her behalf in the event of mental incapacitation, if such policies are available in this jurisdiction. While I certainly wouldn't want Mariam to have to end her life any earlier than she felt she had to, I would also respect Mariam's patient autonomy, and her desire to avoid extreme suffering and to select the medical option she feels is best for her. As her physician, it's not my place to persuade or dissuade Mary on a medical procedure, but rather to provide her with all the evidence and legal options available to her at this time. When I feel Mary is fully informed and had a chance to discuss it with her family, I would allow Mary to make her decision and I would respect the decision she reached **(summary).**

DISCUSSION: In this scenario, the pressing issue is the patient's well-being and quality of life as it related to her desire to seek medically-assisted dying due to suffering from ALS. However, she feels that she may be forced to end her life sooner than she wanted because of a current law in place. Your role in the scenario is her physician and you need to counsel Mariam on options based on the literature. You want to remain objective and non-judgmental, as end-of-life options are a deeply personal. You would not want to jump to conclusions or make generalizations one way or the other. Saying that Mariam should just end her life and not take the chance can be viewed as hasty and insensitive, especially without knowing the current stage of her disease. Likewise, saying that she should just take her chances and wait as long as possible is not respecting the patient's wishes to not have to endure suffering from the disease. A good answer would demonstrate that there is no easy answer and that multiple considerations must be taken into account, including when Mariam was diagnosed and the length of time she has been living with disease, her rate of decline, amount of suffering, possible treatment options to prolong life and alleviate pain, and the wishes of the patient and her family. You must demonstrate your ability to recognize both sides and to consider multiple factors. You should not persuade or dissuade the patient, but rather educate and fully inform them, so that they can make the decision that's best for them.

Station #12: Scenario-based Question

You are new graduate student in a busy research lab. You notice your supervisor, Professor Neville, approach one of your fellow graduate students who is an international student from the Middle East (Jacob). Professor Neville asks Jacob to participate in a research study on adapting to the "western world". The student is shy, and you notice that the student seems to appear uncomfortable with the request and doesn't seem to really want to participate, but reluctantly agrees. After the professor leaves, the student confides in you that they would prefer not to do the study, but felt they had no choice because the supervisor asked and he didn't want to have a bad relationship with Professor Neville. What would you do in this situation?

Theme(s): ethical dilemma, professional boundaries, conflict resolution

BAD: I would stay out of it; it's none of my business. This is between the student and the professor **(deferment of responsibility, not acknowledging pressing issue of research ethics violations taking place within lab).** Additionally, the professor is also my supervisor, so I do not think it would be appropriate to cross any boundaries and potentially ruin our working relationship **(only considering one's interest, does not propose solutions).**

GOOD: In this scenario, I am a graduate student who witnesses an interaction between a fellow grad student and a professor. The professor asks the student (who is an international student) to participate in a research study about adapting to the "western world". I observe that the student seems reluctant to participate, but he ultimately agrees and then later confides in me that he doesn't really want to but felt pressured to do so, in order to maintain a good relationship with the professor **(recap).** This raises an ethical issue about participant consent and coercion. There are clear ethical guidelines that indicate proper participant recruitment and consent, and that there should be no coercion or power imbalance from the researcher and participant. The professor is in a position of power and, as a result, the student did not feel that they had a choice to freely decide if they wanted to participate **(problem/values identification).** I need to ensure the well-being of my fellow graduate student, and that professional boundaries are not crossed within the lab and during the research study **(identifies most pressing issue).** However, I would need to gather more information and I would speak to the student and ask them how they would feel about speaking to the professor about it, if they were uncomfortable, I would encourage them to do so and offer my support to go with them **(information gathering, collegial behavior).** I could also tell the student that I am willing to speak to the professor as well, in order to bring up the ethical issue because, as a research lab, we need to ensure we are acting ethically and in accordance with Research Ethics Board (REB) guidelines. We would also not want to create a negative environment where power imbalances exist and people are made to feel uncomfortable. I would request to meet with the supervisor privately and, in a non-confrontational way, explain that I witnessed the interaction between Jacob and wanted to raise a concern about participant recruitment and consent. I would explain to the professor that Jacob indicated his reluctance with participating in the study and wanted to bring that to the professor's attention, as perhaps he wasn't aware of this. If the professor acknowledges the issue and speaks to Jacob about it and allows Jacob to freely decide, then no further action is necessary. If the professor brushes off the issue and pushes to have Jacob participate, then I would remind the professor that he is a role model and he is mentoring the next generation of researchers and, as such, it is important to set a good example. If he still persisted, then I would inform the professor that I believe this is an ethical violation and that I would need to report it to the university's research ethics board if the professor persists. Furthermore, I understand that such an action might damage my working relationship with this professor but I'm confident that I will be able to find a new supervisor given the circumstance **(if then/solutions).**

DISCUSSION: In this scenario, the main issue is respect for the right of the fellow graduate student to decide if they would like to participate in a study or not, and to do so independently and free from coercion. The applicant should not avoid the issue after witnessing the exchange, especially as they are aspiring researchers themselves and need to act ethically and accordingly. They should also not encourage the other student to feel like they are obligated to comply for fear of repercussions, as this is clearly outlined in the school's ethical guidelines. The "GOOD" answer addresses the issue head-on and seeks to reach a conclusion that will comply with sound ethical research practices and, more importantly, protect the rights and well-being of the vulnerable party (the student) who may feel coerced to participate. The issue must be addressed with the professor who is the supervisor and mentor of future researchers, as this would not want to be passed off as acceptable practice. If the professor acknowledges the issue and makes efforts to correct it, then the problem is solved. If the professor brushes it off, then it's important to remind the professor that he is setting the example for his trainees. If he still refuses to right the situation, then involving the research ethics board would be necessary, even if it may temporarily impact the student. Questions like these are designed to see if you are willing to do the right thing even when doing the right thing may have a temporarily negative personal impact. This is especially critical for professional roles where care of vulnerable parties is frequent.

Station #13: Acting Station/Scenario-based Question

You are a Professor for a 3rd-4th year undergraduate course. As you are marking student essays, you come across one submission that seems suspiciously more advanced than the others. Following a hunch, you begin trying to establish whether this was simply a high-achieving student or a case of plagiarism. After looking into the student's cited sources, you find that they've copied two full pages of a book verbatim, without even using proper quotation or citation for the directly-copied pages. You bring the student in for a one-on-one meeting to discuss this, and she immediately breaks down in tears. She tells you it's her last term before graduation and insists that she's never had any problems like this in the past. Moving forward with a plagiarism case may mean the student cannot graduate at the end of the term, as expected. What do you say to the student, and how do you resolve the situation?

Follow up: You move ahead with the plagiarism case and send the necessary information to the school's Academic Integrity Office. You are invited to sit in on the hearing and contribute to the discussion of consequences. Before bringing the student in, the committee tells you that this is actually not her first time in front of the committee – she'd been found guilty of plagiarism two years prior. How does this influence your decision?

Theme(s): ethical dilemma, possible conflict resolution

Note: Although we have labeled this as an acting station our "BAD" vs. "GOOD" responses are written as if it were a standard question for training purposes. When you practice, try to act out what you would say if this were an acting station.

BAD: I understand this is a tricky situation, and I have an obligation to report this right away. **(judgmental, quick to make a decision).** Immediately following the discovery of plagiarism, I would forward the information to the school's Academic Integrity Office and let them handle it. At this point, what is done is done **(lacks if/then approach, does not explore other solutions).** It is not my problem if this compromises the student's ability to graduate. As a 3rd or 4th year student, I assume the student should have a good understanding of plagiarism and the consequences that follow **(lacks problem solving approach, passing responsibility off to others, lacks professionalism),**

Follow up response (BAD): Clearly this is a student that lacks integrity and does not take her academics very seriously **(judgmental).** I think that in order for the student to truly value the educational system and take responsibility for her actions, we will need to impose severe consequences, for example, suspending her, making a note on her transcripts, or taking away any scholarships she currently possesses **(one-sided solution).**

GOOD: In this scenario, I am a Professor and have come across a student essay that may not be academically honest. In my office, the student has an emotional reaction and expresses fears that an academic integrity hearing might compromise her ability to graduate at the end of the term **(recap).** As the professor, I need to ensure the well-being of my students, while acting in accordance to ethics **(identifies most pressing issue).** The first thing I would want to do is continue my private conversation with the student, to better understand what happened. In a non-confrontational manner, I would ask the student about the main claims of their paper, and where they got the ideas/support for those claims **(non-judgmental perspective, compassion and sensitivity).** I would ask the student if they were familiar with the text that was copied verbatim **(information-gathering).** I want to gauge the student's response to see if there is an indication of foreknowledge of wrongdoing. After this, I would show the copied material from the original text to the student and ask if they realize that they copied this material, without following proper quotation or citation procedures. I would let the student know that this constitutes a violation of academic integrity and provide time for explanations or possible emotional reactions. As I do not yet know if intentional wrong-doing was committed, I would try to be understanding and compassionate, while still maintaining the standards of academic integrity **(professionalism, empathy).** I would ask the student if they'd ever been reported for a violation of academic integrity before, or if anyone had ever spoken to them about their writing. Once the student had explained themselves, I would thank them for their time and let them know that I would follow up within a few days. I would then consult colleagues or the chair of my department for advice, especially if this was my first case of potential plagiarism **(collaboration).** I would also review my school's process for academic integrity hearings and standards of academic integrity, to refresh my memory of the procedure **(information-gathering).** Ultimately, following the advice of others, and with an understanding of the school's policy, I would forward the necessary information to the Academic Integrity Office, knowing that if this was a first offense, the student will receive relatively lenient treatment, and that this will likely not compromise the student's graduation, but will likely result in a zero or reduced mark for the assignment. If it turns out that this was an oversight and the student had genuinely forgotten to cite the work appropriately, then while their grade might be affected, there would be no need to penalize them for plagiarism. If this was intentional, then it needs to be brought to the attention of proper authorities within the university to make sure students advance based on their academic ability not plagiarism **(If/then, solutions).**

Follow up response (GOOD): While this would leave me feeling a bit conflicted about my previous sympathy for the student, since they said they'd not been to an academic integrity hearing before, I would remain as non-judgmental as possible, while still holding firm to the principles of academic honesty **(most pressing issue).** If possible, I would like to gather more information about the previous cases by asking the committee if they can disclose such information to me. While the student was outside the room, I would consult with other members of the group to determine what they thought the best course of action was, since they have a wealth of experience in such matters **(collaboration).** If the punishment fit the violation, I would support the other members of the group in their decision. However, we must remain cognizant that past behavior does not automatically allow us to assume similar behavior in this situation. It is critical that we judge this case on its own and rule out an honest mistake before making a decision. **(maturity of thought)**

DISCUSSION: In this scenario, you are presented with a case of possible plagiarism, and must also navigate tricky emotional territory while considering those who may be directly or indirectly affected by your actions. In the "BAD" response, a rash decision is made, and no concern or consideration for the student is expressed, even though the standards of academic integrity are upheld. In the follow up response, a decision is made based on emotion and assumptions about intent. In the "GOOD" response, the necessary time is taken to fully understand the situation, the steps that follow, and the ramifications of these actions. The student must go in front of the Academic Integrity committee, but this is framed more as a learning experience than a punitive measure. The standards of academic integrity are upheld, while still expressing empathy for the student and avoiding making assumptions. In the follow up response, commitment to ethical principles determines action, not emotion, and deference is made to those most equipped to handle the situation in alignment with the school's regulation, while also learning how to approach such cases in the future.

Summary of scenario-based questions and answers:

In the scenario-based questions presented above, notice how the response is created using the strategies previously discussed. In providing a response, we did not jump to any hasty conclusions based on the preliminary evidence that was presented in the interview question, and even showed some skepticism about what was offered in the prompt. We identified the most pressing issue and allowed that to guide our priorities in addressing the situation. We took the time to gather further evidence prior to acting, and at times, in order to do so, we had to have a private conversation with someone in the scenario. We also considered multiple perspectives and potentialities that could have contributed to the outcomes of the situation prior to formulating an action plan. Eventually, after gathering all of the facts, and after identifying who can directly and indirectly be affected by our actions, we came up with some practical solutions that could be drawn upon in order to solve the problem at hand, only considering the most negative interpretation as a last resort. Since we are not certain about all of the details, all we could do is to describe the various possibilities that can arise and discuss how we would approach each of them. This requires the use of a lot of "if this...then that" statements. Eventually, the solutions that we drew upon were the ones that were the most legal, ethical, scientifically sound, and more importantly, the ones that caused the least amount of harm to the individuals involved in the scenario.

Personal and Quirky Type Questions

Personal and quirky type interview questions can be found on MMIs, MPIs, and traditional or panel interviews. These include questions about your past experiences, your motivation for pursuing the field that you have chosen, and "tell me about a time when..." type questions. This category includes questions such as: "Tell me about a time when you had to act as a leader", or "tell me about a time when you had to show compassion to someone you didn't know".

Station #14: Personal Question

Tell me about a time when you came into conflict with a superior. How did you resolve this problem?

BAD: The one time I had a conflict with a superior was during my time at a clinic where I worked as an administrator. I had a boss that was incredibly rude, controlling, and unprofessional. He was truly not competent to manage the clinic **(unprofessional, red flag)**. My role was to greet the patients coming into the clinic and register them into the system. However, my boss would often tell me my work was not done well and would suggest I get retrained. I felt so embarrassed during our last conversation, I finally decided to defend myself, and shouted back that I knew what I was doing, and that my boss should trust me **(lacks problem-solving skills, unprofessional approach)**. Unfortunately, my boss did not take this well, and decided to let me go. I do not regret what I did **(lacks accountability)**. I am happy I stood my ground and told my boss off, as it was much needed and long overdue **(does not address take-aways and future application)**.

GOOD: While working on a research project as a graduate student, my supervisor and I had some disagreements about the way our data should be presented in our poster presentation during a conference. Although this was not a major conflict, we did have differences in our approaches and this required some time to resolve. I decided to set up a time to discuss the concern with my supervisor in private **(information gathering, problem solving)**. Once at the meeting, in a very professional and respectful manner, I explained my concerns and allowed my supervisor to take the lead in explaining why he felt so strongly about his approach. It was important to listen to his views because I understood that he is certainly more experienced than I am when it comes to the field and, perhaps, I may have missed something important **(seeking to understand, professional, taking responsibility)**. After listening to his rationale and ideas, I was certainly influenced and, although I provided my perspective, rationale, and evidence for why I thought a different approach was needed, at the end of the meeting I was able to see the shortcoming in my approach and luckily this was corrected prior to the presentation. We eventually came to a new consensus and drew upon a hybrid approach that integrated both of our ideas and perspectives **(solution, compromise)**. This was a great learning experience for me as it taught me a valuable lesson about how to resolve disagreements with colleagues and supervisors **(take-a-ways)**. Moving forward, I will certainly resolve conflicts in a professional manner, and always seek to understand the perspective of others first before making any rash decisions, so I can continue to grow as an individual and as a professional **(future application)**.

DISCUSSION: Your response to personal questions must be unique to your own personal experiences. Therefore, while there are no set formulas, you can follow a coherent structure when formulating your response to these types of questions. One that identifies the experience or problem, indicates any resolutions, highlights the lessons learned, and how these lessons can be applied in the future. In the "BAD" response, you will notice that the candidate is speaking in an unprofessional manner about their last boss. The candidate takes no accountability for their action and does not showcase the ability to take feedback without being defensive or to resolve conflicts. The candidate does not address what the experience taught him or her, and how they will use this experience to become a better person. However, in the "GOOD" response, the candidate clearly identifies a conflict and approaches it with an open mind. The candidate acknowledges that his or her views may be misguided due to lack of experience and explicitly indicates that they are going to seek feedback from the supervisor before providing their own views. Lastly, the candidate demonstrates their ability to learn from mistakes and to use a sound strategy when resolving conflicts with superiors in the future.

Station #15: Quirky Question

If you could gain any superpower, what superpower would you want to have?

BAD: A super-power I would want to gain is the ability to fly. Flying seems super cool. Additionally, I would love to travel all over the world, and flying would make it super simple and efficient **(superficial, cliché, addresses a challenge that has already been solved with the advent of planes, lacks personability, informal language).**

GOOD: This is an interesting question. It reminds me of when we were kids and we used to talk about superheroes and superpowers. Even as an adult now, my answer would be the same as when I was a child. If I could gain a superpower with a snap of a finger, I would like to have the ability to time travel. I would think this would be the most amazing experience, because you get to really have insight into how things were in a certain historical period or how things will be in the future **(offers an explanation).** Of course, "with great power comes great responsibility", so I would be sure to use my powers fairly and ethically **(social responsibility).** That said, it would simply be fantastic to be able to travel to the past or future because, for example, you would get the chance to meet some very interesting historical figures that we only get to read about in books. I would be traveling back in time a lot to speak to various historical figures and experience important historical moments in person. Getting the opportunity to witness such moments will allow me to understand things far better than I could if I simply read history books that may have been altered by the authors' biases over time. I would gain knowledge into cultures, governance, and various social issues. This newly-gained knowledge will surely come in handy during my interactions with people from different parts of the world, or from different generations **(future application)**. For these reasons, time travel would be my ideal superpower **(summary)**.

DISCUSSION: Quirky questions can take you in any direction, and thus might seem trickier to navigate. However, ensuring that you do not answer a superficial question with a superficial answer is the best strategy. In the "BAD" response, the candidate answered the question with a cliché response. The candidate did not personalize the answer and did not provide any explanations, and spoke in a very unprofessional manner, overall. However, in the "GOOD" response, the candidate discussed the interesting challenge of time travel and its implications. The candidate further indicated that he/she would only use such powers in a socially responsible manner to learn from historical moments and to improve their knowledge in the process.

Summary of Personal and Quirky Type Questions

When it comes to personal type questions, you simply need to know yourself very well and reflect on your past experiences. One of the toughest personal type questions that you can be asked is, "why do you want to become a doctor/dentist/etc.?" This requires honesty and sincerity. You need to reflect on this question for a long time and come up with genuine reasons behind your motivation. Visit our blog post at the following URL to learn how to learn how to answer this challenging question:

https://bemoacademicconsulting.com/blog/how-to-answer-the-interview-question-why-do-you-want-to-become-a-doctor

Quirky type questions are intended to trip you up and the interviewer is supposed to get a real sense of your personality. Therefore, if you get caught off guard, take a deep breath, smile, and fall back on your training. These questions are less about your answers and more about how you genuinely react to such unexpected questions. Above all, don't forget to show your personality and enjoy a lighthearted moment during your interview.

Writing and Quote Stations

Station #16: Written response

This is a writing station, when you hear the buzzer, enter the room and type your response on the provided computer inside the room: Briefly explain the last argument you had with a close friend. How did you resolve the argument?

BAD: The last fight I had with a friend ended badly **(negative opening, jumps to conclusion).** I have been friends with Sam for over 10 years, and we have been close. However, ever since last summer, Sam and I became distant, because Sam kept spending too much time with his other friends **(lack maturity).** I was the bigger person and attempted to come to a resolution, but obviously Sam was far too busy to care **(self-congratulatory, lacks problem solving).** In the end, I realized I don't need friends like Sam **(displays arrogance, the example provided lacks depth of thought or serious consideration).**

GOOD: The last argument I had with a friend was a growing experience **(positive introduction).** My friend Jessica and I have been friends for over 10 years. In that time, we established effective ways to reconcile, should either of us be angry with each another **(maturity, ability to communicate).** One summer, I realized that Jessica became distant. Of course, this made me upset, and I mistakenly approached her in an accusatory tone for neglecting our friendship without first gathering more information. Jessica, in turn, became upset and stopped talking to me. However, I was not willing to let one misunderstanding get in the way of our friendship. I wanted to see what was going on with Jessica – perhaps she was going through some personal issues and I needed to support her before making any conclusions **(compassion).** Therefore, I approached Jessica again and asked her to have a conversation with me, so I could gather more information. After talking to Jessica, I realized that Jessica's family was struggling financially, and this was the reason she had been distant lately. I apologized to Jessica for being judgmental earlier and offered to support her **(problem solving)**. What I learned from this experience is that the best way to resolve any conflict is to remain non-judgmental and gather as many facts as possible before making any conclusions. Someone might be upset due to other factors unknown to me and if I don't gather more information, I might mistakenly assume that their emotions are directed at me **(take-a-way lesson[s])**. This is a skill I have continued to refine over time and will continue to apply in my future **(future application)**.

DISCUSSION: In this question, the candidate was asked to write about a conflict with a close friend. In the "BAD" response, the candidate takes a very negative and judgmental approach. The candidate does not display accountability, blames her friend, and lacks maturity. However, in the "GOOD" response, the candidate takes responsibility for her actions and admits that she may have been judgmental at first. The candidate showcases a problem-solving approach and with a focus on what she learned. Lastly, the candidate highlights the lessons gained from this experience and discusses how she would use this knowledge in the future.

Station #17: Quote

"Education is the kindling of a flame, not the filling of a vessel." – Socrates

What does this quote mean to you? Go inside the room and discuss your thoughts with the interviewer.

BAD: It is very obvious that Socrates is essentially saying that education is required for you to be successful **(quick judgment)**. I think those that are not successful clearly lack education **(inappropriate response)**. Thus, I wish to continue my studies, so I can become a rich and successful individual **(motivated by self-interests).**

GOOD: A quote by Socrates can be interpreted in many different ways, and this can be possibly influenced by your upbringing and/or current social environment **(remains nonjudgmental).** However, for myself, I believe that the first part, "education is the kindling of the flame", can suggest that education, be it learning formally, in an academic setting, or through your personal experiences, can truly motivate as referenced by the "kindling flame" – that is, lighting a fire of inspiration **(deconstructs the quote).** For example, when I was back-packing through Europe, I came across a French writer, who taught me the importance of story-telling. Through this experience I became drawn to story- tellers, looking for ways they attempted to engage with the audience, and ways they drew on different emotions. This entire experience motivated me to learn more about history and also allowed me to appreciate the history of story-tellers and their role in singlehandedly taking on one of the most monumental aspects of maintaining cultural rituals and traditions **(provides a personal example).** The second part of the quote states, "not the filling of a vessel". For this part, I feel that perhaps Socrates is suggesting that information learned or gained is not simply a means to an end. The vessel can be representative of our brain, and how much we can observe. If gaining knowledge is not simply to fill up our brain, then perhaps that can suggest that there is always room to learn, always room to grow **(deconstructs the second part of the quote).** An example of this was in first year as an undergrad, as a studious individual, I felt that I already had the most effective studying habits in place. However, when I became overwhelmed with the workload, I quickly had to get involved in a study group **(provides an example, showcases ability to collaborate).** Through the process, I learned of other ways to interpret knowledge and to truly understand, such as presenting key ideas to a group about a topic you're unfamiliar with – something that forced me to condense ideas and learn more thoroughly and effectively throughout the process **(highlights take-aways, showcases conflict resolution skills).** In summary, in this quote, Socrates suggests that, education is meant to spark one's interest in learning more without any limitations or end goal in mind (**summary**).

DISCUSSION: For this station you are asked to interpret a quote. Understandably, a quote can be interpreted in many ways that are different, but still good. The strategy is how you choose to deconstruct and what you use to support your opinion. In the 'BAD' response, you will see the candidate is quick to draw to one singular conclusion. The candidate does not use examples to support their claim. Additionally, the candidate would be flagged for stating inappropriate claims that can be viewed as disrespectful. On the other hand, you will notice that in the 'GOOD' response, the candidate remains open to the concept of the quote. The candidate then deconstructs the quote and supports each claim through an example. The use of personal example is effective as the candidate showcases conflict resolution, collaboration, and highlights what they learned and connects it to their future.

Summary of writing/quote stations

Writing stations can take many forms. They could be a quote, a personal-type question, or a scenario-based question. Alternatively, you may be asked to read a brief article and answer a few related questions under timed conditions. Your overall strategy for these station does not change. Simply follow the BeMo strategies we discussed earlier, and you'll be able to answer any type of writing station. It goes without saying but you must pay extra attention to your grammar and spelling, even if the instructions might claim that your grammar and spelling is not important, because an evaluator is more likely to enjoy a well-written response versus one that's full of typos and hard to follow. After all, this is a test of your communications skills.

Drawing and Building Stations

Station #18: Picture Prompts/video prompts

Please enter the room and describe the image below to the interviewer (or another candidate) in detail, so that they may be able to reproduce it as closely as possible without looking at the image.

BAD: This is very simple and straightforward. You should have no problem with quickly reproducing this image **(lacks empathy for the drawer who has never seen the picture).** I want you to draw an image of two box-like figures **(no overall background or recap to orient the other individual).** The first figure is a rectangle, and smaller than the second square. The second square is attached to it at the bottom right and appears to be bigger. The figures are simply outlined, and you should now have the image **(lacks details and clear instructions about size, position on the paper, color, etc.).**

GOOD: In this station, I have been given an image and was instructed to describe it to you so you can reproduce it without looking at the image **(recap).** I think we can accomplish this task pretty well if we communicate clearly with each other. Therefore, as I describe the image, if at any point you have any questions, feel free to ask me to pause and provide further clarification (**underscores the value of communication in this station**). First, I need to ensure that you have the following materials: standard 8 x 11 paper, a black pen or pencil, and a ruler. Let me know once you have those items. If any of these items have not been provided to you let me know so I can adjust my instructions. Since the figures are geometric, we can easily use the XY Cartesian coordinate system. Just so you have an overall idea of what we're drawing, the image contains two geometric shapes, one rectangle and one square. These shapes are connected, with the rectangle oriented horizontally on top, and the square on the bottom, but hanging off to the right of the rectangle. Don't worry, I'm going to walk you through the details of this. First hold your 8 x 11 paper vertically. To construct an XY Cartesian coordinate system, you will first need to draw a line on the left side of the page going down vertically that will be our Y axis. At the bottom of that line, draw another line to the right horizontally, this will be our X axis. At the point where both these points meet, that is our origin, label that 0 (**referencing a coordinate system**). Let me know once you have completed that or if you have any questions before we continue (**collaborative approach**). Now please number both the X and Y axis by dividing them to 1 cm segments, creating 5 segments horizontally and 5 vertically – so, 5x5 cm – labeled 1-5, beginning at the zero and working up and then from zero to the right. Please let me know when you've completed this. I am now going to provide you with specific points on the coordinate system that we will later use to create our two objects. First find X0 and Y2 (so, over 0 and up 2 cm) and label that as point "A". The second point is X3, Y2, label that B. Now with a straight black line connect A to B. Third point, X3, Y4, label that C, and then connect B to C. Fourth point, X0, Y4, label that D, and connect with a straight line to C and back to A. You should now have a rectangle. Now for the second figure: mark a point at X2, Y0, label that E. Mark a point at X4, Y0, label that F, and connect E to F. Mark a point at X4 and Y2, label that G. Go ahead and connect F to G. Our final point is H, please mark a point at X2, Y2. Ensure to connect G to H and finally H to E. This should give you a square. What you should have is two figures, one a rectangle, and the second a square which is connected to the bottom right part of the first rectangle. Let me know if you have any questions or need me to clarify **(summary).**

DISCUSSION: We intentionally provided a simple drawing here for training purposes. Note that you may receive a much more complicated image and you have to use your discretion when you are describing the image to the drawer. Furthermore, you may be at the receiving end of the instructions. If that happens and you notice that the instructor is not following a coherent system, teach them the use of the Cartesian coordinate system, if appropriate, and ask them to clarify at each step (note, while the Cartesian coordinate system works well for straight-lined geometric figures, one of its key limitations is circles; if you're presented with an image that contains a circle, you can reference the hours on an analog clock to indicate where various points or lines should align with the circle). This shows again that you understand the value of collaboration with others. In the "BAD" response, you will notice that the candidate rushes in and provides vague instructions. The candidate also assumes that the other individual understands what is being said and does not clarify. In the "GOOD" response, the candidate provides a systematic system for reproducing the image and slows down the instructions and collaborates with the drawer, repeatedly asking the other individual whether they understand the instructions and whether they require further clarification. The use of the Cartesian coordinate system relies on numbers, eliminating guess work and inaccuracy. Lastly the candidate provides an overall explanation of the shapes to ensure that the drawer has reproduced the right image.

Policy-type Questions

Station #19: Policy-type Question

There are currently talks of implementing a $10 patient fee, not covered by any insurance nor government health plans, for those going to their family doctors and those seeking care at the ER. What are your views about this idea?

BAD: I think that a $10 fee would go a long way to help the hospital and the doctors, so I would certainly agree with this policy **(one-sided, rushes to an opinion)**. A fee would also keep patients from seeing the doctor when it is not necessary, and this will help the doctors as they are often overwhelmed. Lastly, the money could be used to get new equipment for the hospital, which is great for the hospital staff and the patients **(only considers pros and neglects the possible negative impacts on patients)**.

GOOD: I can understand why such a fee would be introduced. This would essentially act as a deterrent fee and make individuals re-consider when it is essential to go to the doctor or the hospital and when it is not. The healthcare system is definitely under a lot of financial stress, especially as a result of our aging population and the increased need for services. There are pros and cons associated with such a policy **(demonstrates broad awareness)**.

First, as I already mentioned, this $10 fee would act as a deterrent and perhaps prevent unnecessary visits to the doctor's office and the ER. This would take some of the burden off of our healthcare system and generate funds, which can be used towards improving our healthcare system; but, of course, this hypothesis will need to be objectively validated **(pros)**.

With that said, the problem with such a policy arises when the deterrent fee acts as a barrier to seeking care for those who come from a lower socioeconomic strata of society. For some, a $10 fee may be a major demand and, as a result, they may not seek out help from their doctors even in times when it is genuinely necessary **(considers the cons).** This can end up creating more costs for the healthcare system in the long run because, as conditions become more chronic over time, the cost required to appropriately address such health conditions increases **(considers consequences, future application).** Therefore, we may be saving in doctor visits in the short run through such a fee, but it can end up costing us a lot later down the line.

I do not believe implementing a deterrent fee as a means of reducing the stress on the healthcare system is a good idea. We can explore other avenues to reduce the burden on our system. For instance, we can educate the general public about the appropriate use of healthcare services and when it is required to seek out help from doctors or the ER. As well, implementing or encouraging tools such as tele-health and/or web-health services, where individuals can contact a healthcare professional for advice over the Internet, are great examples of how technologies can be used to educate the population. We should also be more focused on preventative measures as a long-term solution to dealing with the demands that our healthcare system is facing. This requires mass education of the population about a healthy and active living lifestyle, which in the long run will reduce the total number of individuals who will need to seek out medical care throughout their life **(calculated opinion, offers alternate solutions).**

DISCUSSION: A great response needs to consider all sides of the argument and all parties involved. In the "BAD" response, you will notice that the candidates rush to agree with the policy, only considering doctors in the process. The candidate also seeks to support the opinion by drawing on the benefits of the policy, and only considering the benefits of one party. Importantly, the candidate does not consider the implications of such a policy on patients, whereas patient-centered concerns need to be a fundamental part of any approach. In the "GOOD" response, the candidate addresses the rising concerns within healthcare. Additionally, the response addresses both the pros and cons of the policy, again with all respective parties in mind. The opinion is then fully supported by the rationale provided. Finally, the candidate provides a rational alternative with better long-term impacts for patients, doctors, and the entire healthcare system, accounting for all directly and indirectly involved parties.

Station #20: Policy-type Question

What are your thoughts on legalizing recreational marijuana?

BAD: I think whether we legalize recreational marijuana or not, people will still indulge in it **(poor introduction)**. However, I do not think we should legalize it as it is unsafe and will further encourage criminal activities amongst the youth **(judgmental, only focuses on the cons)**. Lastly, I do not personally indulge in any sort of drugs and do not feel the need to ever do so, thus it should not be legalized **(does not showcase awareness of topic or considers multiple perspectives)**.

GOOD: Legalizing recreational marijuana is a controversial global topic. More recently, certain states and countries have reformed their policies and legalized recreational marijuana **(good introduction, showcases awareness of topic)**. There are many advantages and disadvantages when exploring this topic. In terms of advantages, we can consider multiple perspectives. For example, when considering those individuals that indulge in recreational marijuana, often these individuals access such substances in dangerous environments that may compromise their safety. Legalizing marijuana will reduce the risk and harm potentially caused to these individuals **(prioritizing well-being of potentially vulnerable parties)**. This can also combat the current opioid crisis by bringing in alternative pain management options. Secondly, when considering those individuals currently incarcerated for possession or selling of marijuana, this new policy can help in reducing the incarceration rates. Research suggests that most of these offenders leave prison in a worse state than they would be in if they were not imprisoned, mainly because they become exposed to more severe criminals. Not only is this costly for the community, but this will allow authorities to focus on criminal activity that is most consequential. Additionally, legalizing marijuana can allow the government to better control the substance distribution and thus generate profit which can go back to the communities **(considering pros, explores multiple perspectives)**. On the other hand, there are many disadvantages to this policy. For example, substance abuse is still harmful, and there is research that suggests long-term abuse can lead to anxiety or schizophrenic disorders. Additionally, regulating recreational marijuana will be a challenging task, and can compromise the safety of the community. Lastly, legalizing marijuana can be harmful to the youth and even children as there will be a greater access to the substance **(cons)**. When it comes to legalizing marijuana, I do support the policy **(clearly states their position on the topic)**. However, I think we need to better educate the community, and even more so the youth, on the use and abuse of the substance. Additionally, we need to ensure we have better regulations in place to not compromise the safety of the public. Lastly, we need to do further research on the long-term effects of marijuana abuse to ensure we are prepared **(provides modifications, considers future application)**.

DISCUSSION: The policy question presented is certainly controversial and a hot topic. You will notice in the "BAD" response, the individual offers an opinionated response, one that focuses mainly on their own interests. Additionally, they only consider the disadvantages of the policy. Lastly, the candidate does not propose alternatives to the policy after rejecting it. However, you will notice that the candidate in the "GOOD" response explores both advantages and disadvantages for multiple perspectives. Additionally, the candidate, clearly states their position on the policy after discussing both pros and cons, and then explores ways to approach some of the issues discussed.

Summary of policy type questions

When it comes to policy type questions, much like scenario-based questions, there is a systematical way in which you can approach them in order to formulate a strong and appropriate response. Notice in our answers above, we did not jump to a hasty conclusion and we did not take a side on any issues prematurely. We started with a basic introduction that lets the interviewers know that we are aware of the issues. Then, we discussed pros and cons associated with the proposed policy, giving patient-centered arguments first, prior to providing doctor-centered arguments. Then, once we had presented both sides of the argument, we either took a side or provided a unique solution to the problem at hand that was completely different from the ideas proposed in the policy. This allows you to further show your awareness of the issues and set yourself apart from other candidates by providing a unique, creative solution.

Now that we have outlined our step-by-step strategies and have provided you with multiple examples of GOOD versus BAD responses, it is time to apply what you learned in real practice. The next chapter, which includes two sets of MMI practice questions, will allow you to test what you learned by applying the BeMo strategies. Before you start, go back and re-read the previous chapter first. Here is what we want you to do: For the first set, do *not* time yourself, rather go over each scenario and practice by identifying the question types and applying the BeMo framework for acing any MMI question outlined in *Chapter VI: Pre-mortem: 18 Proven Strategies to Prepare for and Ace Any MMI Question* before formulating your response. Then, get expert feedback from a mature professional (or sign up for a BeMo MMI prep program), so you can learn from your mistakes. It is critical that you do not rely on feedback from your peers or students in the field because, by definition, students, even those accepted into your program of choice, are not qualified to provide mentorships and often have not yet developed the insight necessary to accurately assess your performance. This is why BeMo almost never hires students in training as admissions experts.

Once you are completely satisfied and confident that you got all the questions in the first practice test, it's time to take your second practice test. This time however, we want you to do it a bit differently by timing and recording yourself. Treat the practice like an actual interview by setting yourself up in a quiet area so you are not disturbed, and even at the same time as your scheduled interview (if you know it in advance), while wearing the same outfit you will be wearing for the interview date. We recommend timing yourself as follows: 2 minutes to read each prompt and 4 minutes to answer each station. We recommend 4 minutes even if you are going to have 8 minutes during your actual interview, because we want to ensure that you are able to provide a concise answer. Lastly, answer all questions in one sitting to simulate. After your mock interview, review your responses and our formula to find out what you think you did well and what think you did poorly. Then, as always, seek expert feedback.

Chapter XIII

2 Full-Length Practice MMI Question Sets

B elow, you will find two MMI practice interviews. As previously discussed, for effective practice you need to simulate the environment as much as possible. Things to consider prior to taking the mock interviews include: dressing professionally, setting up a quiet room where you will not be disturbed, and most importantly timing yourself. Use a stopwatch or an online timer. Give yourself 2 minutes to read the station prompt, and 4 minutes to respond. Again note that we intentionally want you to reduce your response time to 4 minutes instead of 8 minutes because we have found that most students struggle with being concise. This is the same exact time constraints we use with our students in our MMI prep programs.

Mock MMI Interview #1

MMI Station 1

You are shopping in a store when you see an elderly woman in distress, frantically looking around as though she has lost something. You approach her gently and ask if she is okay. She says that she thinks she's set her purse down somewhere and can't find it. She begins crying, saying that her money for the month and her newly-refilled prescription medications are in the purse, and quickly becomes extremely distressed and incomprehensible. She leans on your arm for support, as if she is about to fall over. How do you handle this situation?

What type of MMI station is this?

What type of theme(s) can you identify?

What's the most pressing issue?

What are the missing facts?

Who is directly and indirectly involved?

What are some possible solutions using if/then strategy?

MMI Station 2

If you could go back to relive any memory, which would it be and why?

Please go inside and discuss with the interviewer.

<u>What type of MMI station is this?</u>

<u>What's the most pressing issue?</u>

<u>What is the best strategy?</u>

MMI Station 3

Mr. Smith is a new patient to your clinic. You go into the room to introduce yourself, and Mr. Smith immediately states, "You're the doctor? I would really prefer to see the male doctor." How would you handle this situation? Please discuss your approach with the interviewer inside the room.

<u>What type of MMI station is this?</u>

<u>What type of theme(s) can you identify?</u>

<u>What's the most pressing issue?</u>

What are the missing facts?

Who is directly and indirectly involved?

What are some possible solutions using if/then strategy?

MMI Station 4

You have just been given an image to observe. Please go inside and describe the image so the interviewer can reconstruct it. You are only allowed to use your words for this exercise.

<u>What type of MMI station is this?</u>

What's the most pressing issue?

What is the best strategy?

MMI Station 5

Acting station: You have just spent an extended period of time with your patient, Mrs. Fallon, who has a complicated medical history and required a long appointment to address all her medical concerns. As she was leaving the room, she briefly fainted, and you needed to re-evaluate her and help coordinate her transfer to the emergency room. You are now running very behind on your subsequent appointments. You are about to enter the next room to see Mr. Rogers, who your nurse warns you is extremely upset that he has been kept waiting for almost an hour. Walk inside the room and speak to Mr. Rogers.

What type of MMI station is this?

What type of theme(s) can you identify?

What's the most pressing issue?

What are the missing facts?

Who is directly and indirectly involved?

What are some possible solutions using if/then strategy?

MMI Station 6

You are a medical resident just starting a new rotation. Yesterday, you came home from a particularly busy day, from which you needed a good night's sleep to recover. You wake up early with the feeling that you have made a mistake on your last patient. You rush to your computer to check the file and find that instead of prescribing 400 milligrams you wrote 1400 milligrams. What's worse is that the staff physician who must verify and give final approval on any treatment, signed off on the medication, missing the error. You check the guidelines noticing that while this dose is high it is within allowable limits. The record shows the patient was stable during morning rounds. Will you do anything given that the dose appears to be within allowable limits for this medication? Why or why not?

What type of MMI station is this?

What type of theme(s) can you identify?

What's the most pressing issue?

What are the missing facts?

Who is directly and indirectly involved?

What are some possible solutions using if/then strategy?

MMI Station 7

You are an elementary school teacher. Your school board has recently introduced the new health curriculum which, amongst other topics, introduces names for male and female genitalia in the second grade. After school one day, a parent approaches you upset after her daughter repeated what you have taught in class. How would you handle this situation?

<u>What type of MMI station is this?</u>

<u>What type of theme(s) can you identify?</u>

<u>What's the most pressing issue?</u>

What are the missing facts?

Who is directly and indirectly involved?

What are some possible solutions using if/then strategy?

MMI Station 8

You are a resident working on the medical ward. One of the experienced nurses comes to you and puts a sheet of orders in front of you and says, "I already gave the patient this medication, which was recommended by the attending physician and I need you to sign off on it". You haven't examined the patient that day and do not know much about this new patient on the ward. How would you respond?

What type of MMI station is this?

What's the most pressing issue?

What are the missing facts?

Who is directly and indirectly involved?

What are some possible solutions using if/then strategy?

MMI Station 9

It is well known that big Pharmaceutical companies along with their expansive lobby have a huge influence on the medical profession and its education. In your opinion what are the positives and negatives of having the Pharmaceutical companies play a role, if any, within medical educational institutions? If you do not think that Pharmaceutical companies should have any role within medical schools, what steps would you take to remove big interest groups such as Big Pharma out of the education system if given the opportunity?

<u>What type of MMI station is this?</u>

<u>What type of theme(s) can you identify?</u>

<u>What's the most pressing issue?</u>

What are the missing facts?

Who is directly and indirectly involved?

What are some possible solutions using if/then strategy?

MMI Station 10

You are a law student and as part of your "field experience" you are enrolled in a course that involves helping resolve legal issues for elderly people who would not be able to afford a lawyer otherwise. You ask your course supervisor, Morgan, if someone will be looking over your work. You are informed that you must handle these cases completely independently and that this will serve as an excellent learning opportunity. On one hand, you would like to make the most of this opportunity so that you can go on to help others in a future career in law. Also, the elderly people you are helping may not have legal representation otherwise. On the other hand, you worry about performing unsupervised, potentially making a mistake, and you feel guilty about whether you may be taking advantage of a vulnerable population. What would you do in this situation and what, if anything, would you say to Morgan?

<u>What type of MMI station is this?</u>

<u>What type of theme(s) can you identify?</u>

What's the most pressing issue?

What are the missing facts?

Who is directly and indirectly involved?

What are some possible solutions using if/then strategy?

Mock MMI Question Set #2

MMI Station 1

You are the leader of an American cultural and historical club on campus and have had weekly meetings to plan for an upcoming event for July 4th celebrations. In one meeting, you over hear certain members of the club make anti-Semitic and anti-Islamic comments. Further, you also hear comments about the cultural superiority of Americans and how the whole world would be better off if they were just like America. As the president of the club, you pride yourself on being inclusive and celebrating the diversity of Americans and you would not want these views to be associated with your club. What would you say to these individuals who made these comments? How would you handle this situation as the President of the club?

<u>What type of MMI station is this?</u>

<u>What type of theme(s) can you identify?</u>

What's the most pressing issue?

What are the missing facts?

Who is directly and indirectly involved?

What are some possible solutions using if/then strategy?

MMI Station 2

You are the director of a refugee camp and are down to your last tent. There are two families, hungry and shivering, currently waiting for tents. The Sawyer family consists of a grandmother, age 84, and three children, all younger than 2 years old. The Finley family consists of a couple, ages 33 and 31. One of your co-workers insists that the last tent should go to the Finley family because everyone in the Sawyer family is very sick and likely to die soon regardless of whether or not they have a tent. A different co-worker disagrees, insisting that the last tent should go to the Sawyer family because the Finley family has fewer people and is more likely to survive without a tent.

	Sawyer Family	Finley Family
# of members	4 members	2 members
ages	84, 2, 1, and 1	33 and 31
Chance of survival with last tent	55%	95%
Chance of survival without last tent	5%	40%

Consider the table above. Assume that "survival" refers to all members of the family as a unit, that is, assume that the only two possible outcomes are either the entire family surviving or the entire family perishing. Further, assume that there is no way to procure additional tents and that you must make a decision now.

To which family will you give the tent, and why? What will you say to the *other* family?

What type of MMI station is this?

What type of theme(s) can you identify?

What's the most pressing issue?

What are the missing facts?

Who is directly and indirectly involved?

What are some possible solutions using if/then strategy?

MMI Station 3

You are a family physician working in a busy practice comprised of four other (physician) colleagues. One of your colleagues has been your life-long friend since before you started your journey of medical school. As of late, you have noticed they have been evasive, and slowly withdrawing from you and their close circle of family and friends. Today marks the end of the first month of back-to-school season, and prescription counts have been at an all-time high. You have just concluded that one of your patients requires a routine cough and cold medication, only to find that you are unable to locate your prescription pad. You don't think twice and ask one of your colleagues if they are able to assess the patient so that they are able to personally write a prescription. Later in the week, you are required to write a prescription and are unable to locate your triplicate pad—a special prescription pad for Schedule II drugs. You are now growing concerned, as you are very diligent in ensuring your prescription pads are always safe and secured. You find your good friend, to confide in them, but are met with resistance and told that they will connect with you later due to being busy. At the end of the week, you receive a call from a pharmacist in the neighboring town, calling to routinely confirm a triplicate prescription written in your name. You quickly realize the patient is one that you have not seen in the clinic for over one year. You ask the pharmacist to recount the triplicate prescription history and are told that your name has signed off on eight consecutive triplicate prescriptions in the past year. How do you approach this situation?

<u>What type of MMI station is this?</u>

What type of theme(s) can you identify?

What's the most pressing issue?

What are the missing facts?

Who is directly and indirectly involved?

What are some possible solutions using if/then strategy?

MMI Station 4

You are working in a group of 5 on a final research project for school. It's coming up to the deadline and it's your turn to review the paper before submitting it tomorrow. Your group has worked well together and haven't had any issues so far. When you are going through the paper for a final read-through, you realize that a large portion of your best friend's section has been blatantly plagiarized. You are due to hand in the paper tomorrow and don't really have time to rewrite it. What would you do?

<u>What type of MMI station is this?</u>

<u>What type of theme(s) can you identify?</u>

<u>What's the most pressing issue?</u>

What are the missing facts?

Who is directly and indirectly involved?

What are some possible solutions using if/then strategy?

MMI Station 5

You are a first-year resident in the emergency department and have just caught word that there was a violent incident that occurred during your local Pride Parade, resulting in numerous injuries. Understaffed and overwhelmed, you breathe a sigh of relief as you see your mentoring physician walk into the department, ready to be briefed about the situation. You have built up quite the rapport with this attending, as you truly admire his practice, and hope to emulate his skills and mannerisms one day. As you find yourself going through the motions of assessing and triaging each patient, you can't help but notice that the attending is nowhere in sight. As you finish up seeing your final patient, you decide to dedicate your upcoming break to finding your attending, to see if they need a hand, as the ER still appears to be backed up. You didn't have to look very far, seeing as the attending was walking out of the adjacent room. The attending asks if you would like to join them for a quick coffee run for the staff, and you oblige. You proceed in asking the attending if you may join them for their upcoming consults for the night. Your attending nonchalantly discloses that your time may be better spent shadowing another physician, as they had no interest in treating any of the casualties related to the Pride Parade incident. Your attending continues to disclose that the last room they had walked into appeared to have the "first normal-looking patient of the day" until the attending reviewed the patient's file, quickly realizing that the patient was "one of *them*". How do you proceed?

<u>What type of MMI station is this?</u>

What type of theme(s) can you identify?

What's the most pressing issue?

What are the missing facts?

Who is directly and indirectly involved?

What are some possible solutions using if/then strategy?

MMI Station 6

What are your views on a Single Payer Health Care System? Discuss the benefits and drawbacks with the interviewer.

<u>What type of MMI station is this?</u>

<u>What's the most pressing issue?</u>

<u>What is the best strategy?</u>

MMI Station 7

You are the pediatrician of a five-year old boy named Michael. In recent visits, Michael has been saying that he likes to play with Barbies, wear his mother's high heels, and would prefer to wear dresses. Michael has been telling you that he wishes he was a girl and that his name was Michelle. Michael's parents are very concerned with Michael's behavior, in that he is not conforming to the typical male gender roles and they worry about the long-term mental health and well-being of their son, specifically about teasing he gets at school. What would you say to Michael's parents, what would you suggest to Michael's parents on how to handle the situation?

<u>What type of MMI station is this?</u>

<u>What type of theme(s) can you identify?</u>

<u>What's the most pressing issue?</u>

What are the missing facts?

Who is directly and indirectly involved?

What are some possible solutions using if/then strategy?

MMI Station 8

You are a family physician. A patient you know well, Jeanne, comes into your office with the results of a direct-to-consumer genetic test she ordered for herself online. This genetic test determines that she has a gene indicating a specific gene variant that results in a high risk for breast cancer. She is emotionally distraught and is crying in your office. The report contains information about specific genes that are outside your area of knowledge. How do you approach this situation?

What type of MMI station is this?

What type of theme(s) can you identify?

What's the most pressing issue?

185

What are the missing facts?

Who is directly and indirectly involved?

What are some possible solutions using if/then strategy?

MMI Station 9

You are a junior academic researcher. You have been working for four years on a project related to a specific gene in muscular dystrophy. You have written several papers, which are under review but not yet published, and have shared your research findings openly with interested colleagues for collaborations and at conferences. Recently, you heard that a colleague of yours was awarded a very competitive grant for which you had also applied. You find out that the title is extremely similar to your own work related to this gene in muscular dystrophy, and you are concerned that the content of the grant was similar. You were unaware he was working on similar research. You find out that the senior researcher, with whom you share the project and the data, had shared your data with the other researcher to use in the grant. How would you approach this situation?

<u>What type of MMI station is this?</u>

<u>What type of theme(s) can you identify?</u>

What's the most pressing issue?

What are the missing facts?

Who is directly and indirectly involved?

What are some possible solutions using if/then strategy?

MMI Station 10

One Sunday afternoon, as you visit your best friend and her family, her younger sister, Dorine, confides in you that she recently started dating a boy from college. From what she says, it appears she is very happy with this new relationship. She asked you to promise her not to tell her family, and especially her older sister, your best friend. You've always had a trusting relationship with Dorine, but you can't help but question the age gap. You've always known her to be rebellious as a child, and at one point she even got in trouble with authorities. How would you handle this situation?

What type of MMI station is this?

What type of theme(s) can you identify?

What's the most pressing issue?

What are the missing facts?

Who is directly and indirectly involved?

What are some possible solutions using if/then strategy?

Chapter XIV

The Final Secret of 76% of Successful Applicants

We hope you enjoyed the book. Our goal was to teach you everything we know. As promised, we did not hold back. In fact, everything we included in this book is what we teach our students in our MMI prep programs found at BeMoMMI.com. We are confident that the strategies we provided along with deliberate practice is going to help you too. But there is one missing piece of the puzzle we were not able to include in this book. This is what 76% of our successful students use in addition to the book.

Here's what we were not able to include in this book:

Our most successful students also take advantage of our realistic online mock interviews followed by expert feedback. In our experience that's the only way to put the strategies we teach here into practice and internalize them.

Here is exactly how our MMI prep program work in 3 simple steps:

Step #1: It actually all starts with the way we select and train our admissions experts. First, because our consultants can work with us remotely, we look for only the best anywhere in the world. This way we are not limited to a small talent pool in a narrow geographical location. We screen dozens of applicants every month. The application process is rigorous and involves a functional test where we test the applicants' ability as potential admissions experts. Followed by an online interview and assessment. Followed by a panel interview with our senior team including our CEO, Dr. Behrouz Moemeni. Out of all the applicants only 5% get hired.

But it doesn't end there. After new applicants are hired, they receive extensive training from our lead trainers. The rigorous training and monitoring last 6 months. This process either leads to them becoming BeMo certified or they are rejected before they are let go with respect because we only want the very best for our students.

Step #2: We focus on teaching our students specific strategies to answer any type of question, make sound judgments on the spot, manage stress and communicate fluently. We actually want to teach skills that last a lifetime and not some dirty, cheap or quick tricks just to get around the interview.

Step #3: We continuously monitor each student's progress using a proprietary scoring system. We score students on over multiple variables including communication skills, stress levels, eye contact, ethical judgment and so forth. This allows us to have a numeric system of assessment rather than gut feeling. We keep going until our admissions experts are confident that our students are 100% ready for their interviews. You read that right. Some of our programs include unlimited mock interviews plus expert feedback.

That's not all. All of our programs are backed by our 100% satisfaction guarantee and some even include our Get In Or Your Money Back® guarantee.

Now, that's the secret sauce of our MMI prep programs. That's why we are trusted by most applicants. If you are serious about mastering the multiple mini interview and getting into your dream program, go to **BeMoMMI.com** to learn more now. We look forward to working with you!

Chapter XV

Bonus Resources and Free Sample MMI SIM

H ere are some additional resources to help you prepare for your MMI:

Free online mock MMI simulator via access to BeMo's revolutionary InterviewProf™ platform: **BeMoSampleMMI.com**

BeMo's 100 sample MMI questions:

https://bemoacademicconsulting.com/blog/sample-mmi-practice-questions

BeMo's private MMI test prep MasterMind Facebook Group:

https://www.facebook.com/groups/BeMo.MMIPrep.MasterMind/

BeMo's Ultimate Pre-Med Resource Center:

https://bemoacademicconsulting.com/premed-resources

BeMo's MMI prep blog:

https://bemoacademicconsulting.com/blog/category-multiple-mini-interview.html

Made in the USA
Monee, IL
16 September 2021